Starfish K3

Learning Linker

Catalogue Publication Data

Starfish K3 Learning Linker
Author: Angela Llanas / Libby Williams
Pearson Educación de México, S.A. de C.V., 2019
ISBN: 978-607-32-4672-9
Area: ELT
Format: 30.5 x 23.5 cm Page count: 184

Managing Director: Sergio Fonseca ■ **Innovation & Learning Delivery Director:** Alan David Palau ■ **Regional Content Manager - English:** Andrew Starling ■ **Publisher:** Hened Manzur ■ **Content Development:** Catalina Hernández ■ **Content Support:** Silvia Barrientos ■ **Art and Design Coordinator:** Juan Manuel Santamaría ■ **Design Process Supervisor:** Salvador Pereira ■ **Layout:** Berenice Hinojosa ■ **Cover Design:** BrandB/Fenómeno ■ **Interior Design:** BrandB/Fenómeno ■ **Photo Research:** Salvador Pereira ■ **Photo Credits:** Shutterstock ■ **Illustrations:** Ana Elena García, Gerardo Sánchez, Miguel Ángel Chávez, José de Santiago Torices, Mónica Cahué, Sheila Cabeza de Vaca, Víctor Sandoval, Ximena García Trigos

The Publisher wishes to acknowledge the valuable collaboration of **Sophie Angerman**, author of the Mathematics program.

First published, 2019

ISBN PRINT BOOK: 978-607-32-4672-9

Esta obra se terminó de imprimir en abril del 2022 en los talleres de:
Diversidad Gráfica S.A. de C.V.
Privada de Av. 11 #1, Col. El Vergel, Iztapalapa, C.P. 09880,
México, Ciudad de México, Tel. 5426-6386
www.diversidadgrafica.com

Impreso en México. *Printed in Mexico.*

1 2 3 4 5 6 7 8 9 0 - 22 21 20 19

D.R. © 2019 por Pearson Educación de México, S.A. de C.V.
Avenida Antonio Dovalí Jaime #70
Torre B, Piso 6, Colonia Zedec Ed. Plaza Santa Fe
Delegación Álvaro Obregón, México, Ciudad de México, C. P. 01210

www.pearsonelt.com

Pearson Hispanoamérica
Argentina ■ Belice ■ Bolivia ■ Chile ■ Colombia ■ Costa Rica ■ Cuba ■ República Dominicana ■ Ecuador ■ El Salvador ■ Guatemala ■ Honduras ■ México ■ Nicaragua ■ Panamá ■ Paraguay ■ Perú ■ Uruguay ■ Venezuela

Contents

● **Trace, say, and color.**

Phonemic Awareness
Learning to Know

M m

ilk and angoes.

Objective: Recognize and identify words with starting sound /m/.

Color. Follow the code.

Mathematical Thinking

Learning to Know

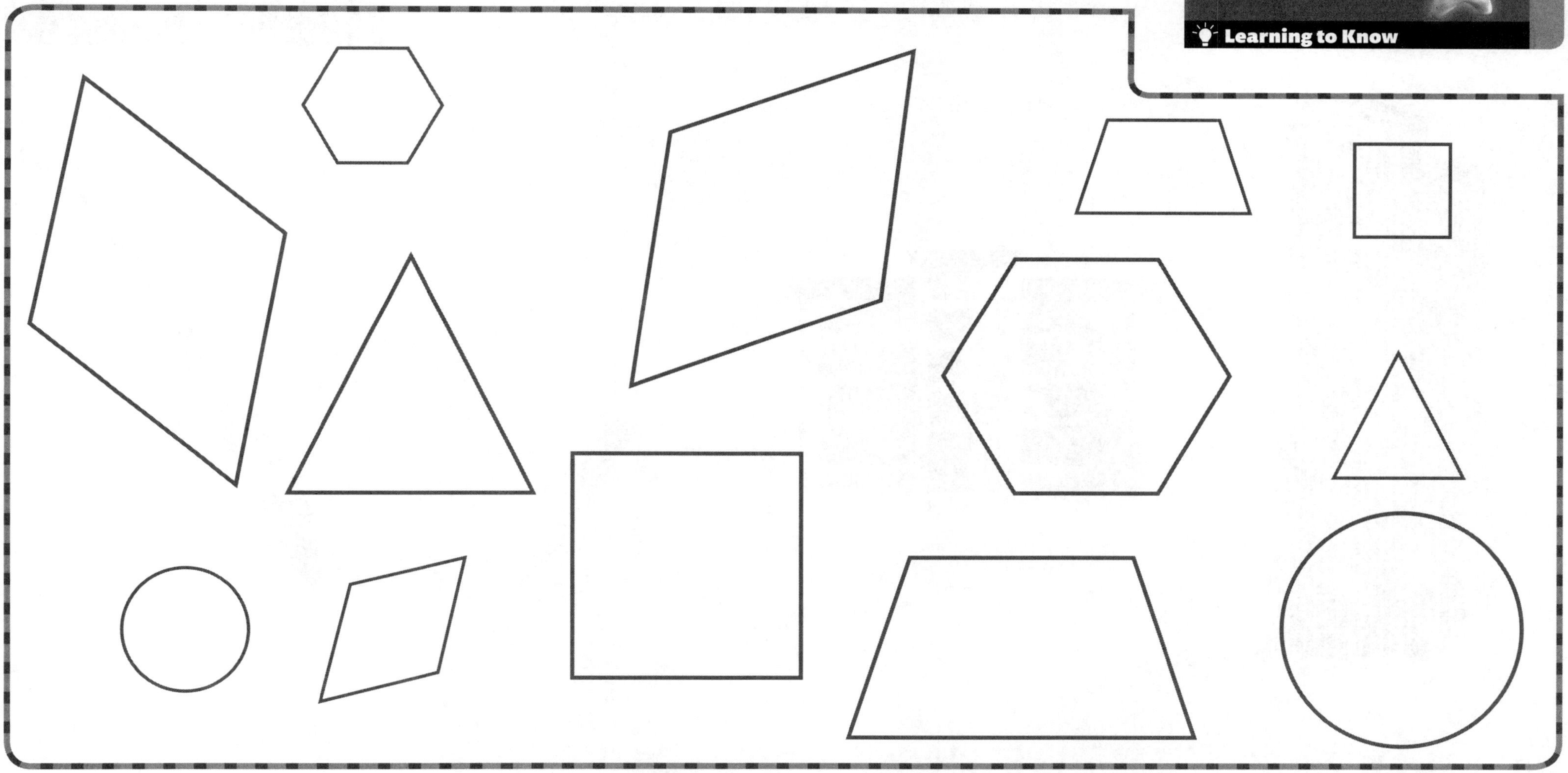

big = red   small = blue

Match the big shapes with the small shapes.

Objectives: Name all basic shapes. Match big and small.

Trace. Circle the letter *m*.

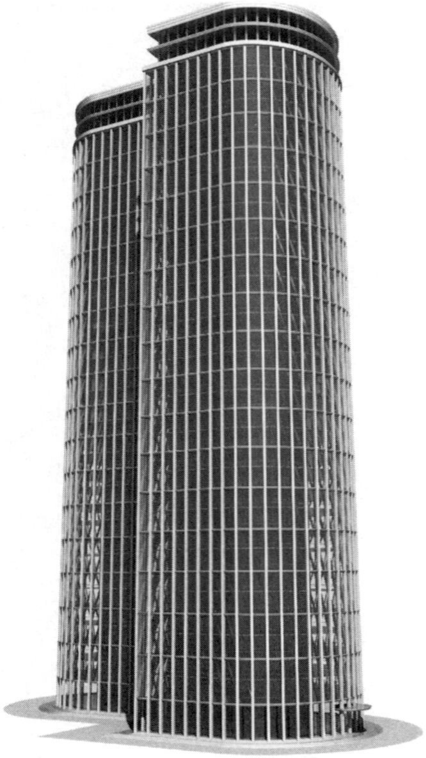

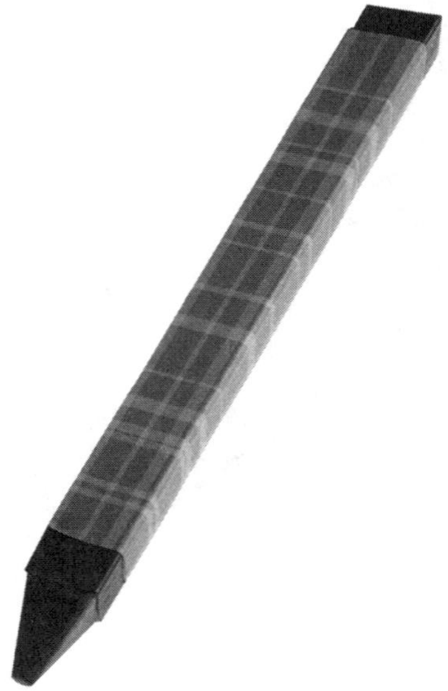

tall short small big

Think!
When do you use the word "medium"?

Write the words below the pictures.

Objectives: Write words to describe. Recognize the letter *m*.

- **Work with a partner. Mime and guess the actions.**

Artistic Expression and Appreciation

Learning to Be

- **Color the things you can do.**

Objective: Identify activities.

Self-care

Learning to Do

Color the things you do.

Complete the sentences.

✔ I like to ______________________.

✘ I don't like to ______________________.

Objectives: Reflect on good and bad behavior with friends. Express likes and dislikes.

- **Read the words and circle the *s* sound.**

snake orange squirrel school

- **Color the pictures of the words with the *s* sound.**

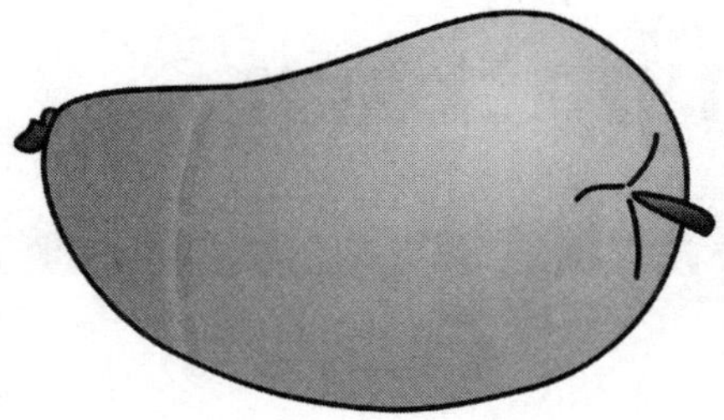

snake squirrel mango school

Objective: Recognize the /s/ sound.

Mathematical Thinking

Learning to Know

Look and complete the patterns.

2 2 3 2 2 3 2 ___ ___ ___ ___

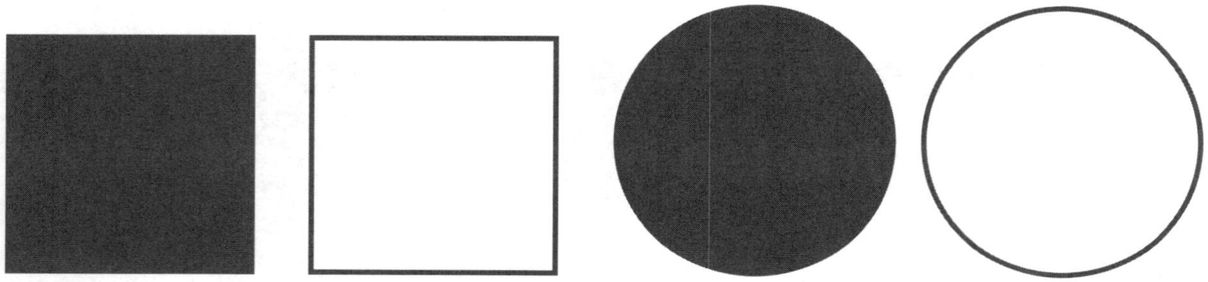 ___ ___

Draw your own pattern.

Objective: Extend and create a simple pattern.

Developmental Writing

Learning to Know

Trace.

S s S s S s S s S s S s S

Draw two words that begin with *s*. Write them.

Complete the patterns.

Mathematical Thinking

Learning to Know

Do the actions in the patterns.

Objectives: Complete a pattern. Follow a pattern with body movements and expressions.

How do you feel today? Draw your face.

Self-care

Learning to Do

Complete the sentence.

I feel ______________________ today.

Objective: Express how they feel using target language.

Phonemic Awareness

Learning to Know

- Circle the pictures that begin with *m*.

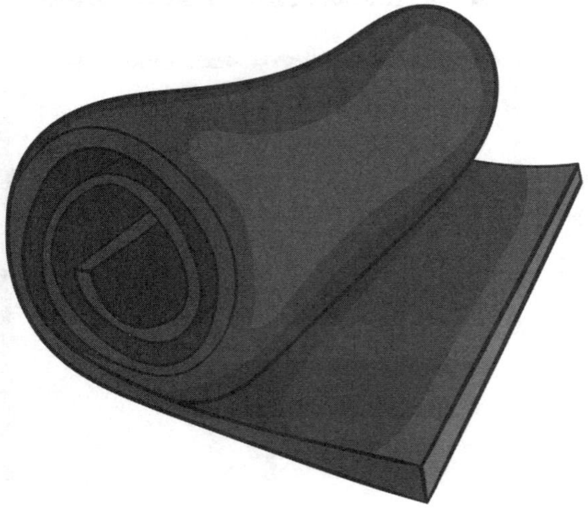

- Cross out the words that begin with *s*.
- Write a word that begins with *S*.

Objectives: Identify beginning sounds /m/ and /s/.

- **Count and color 7 pencils and 10 crayons.**

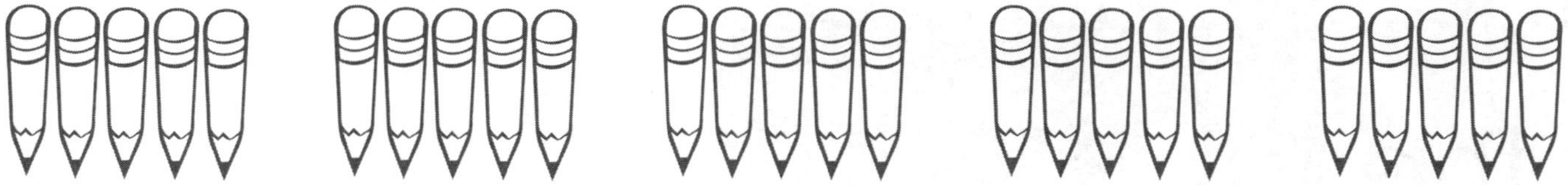

- **Draw dots for each number.**

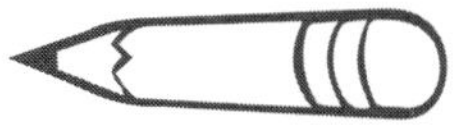 =25

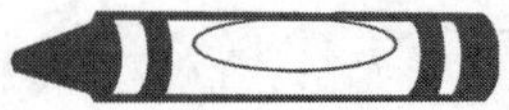 =28

Objectives: Count to 30. Represent an amount with dots on a ten frame.

Developmental Writing

Learning to Know

Where are the children? Trace.

They are in the classroom.

They are on the bus.

Write the words.

Objective: Trace words with letters *m* and *s*.

Read and draw.

Artistic Expression and Appreciation

Learning to Be

My classroom.

My teacher.

My favorite place at school.

Objectives: Take care of different locations at school. Talk about likes and dislikes.

Self-care

Learning to Do

Complete, circle, and draw.

My name is ____________________

____________________.

I like my family.

I like my friends.

I don't like ____________________.

I am 4 5 6 years old.

This is me!

Objectives: Develop their understanding of the concept of self.
Talk about likes and dislikes.

Look and say the words.

Phonemic Awareness

Learning to Know

sun

snake

mat

starfish

Color the picture with the *m* sound.

Objective: Identify letters *m* and *s*.

Mathematical Thinking

Learning to Know

Count, color, and write the number of dots.

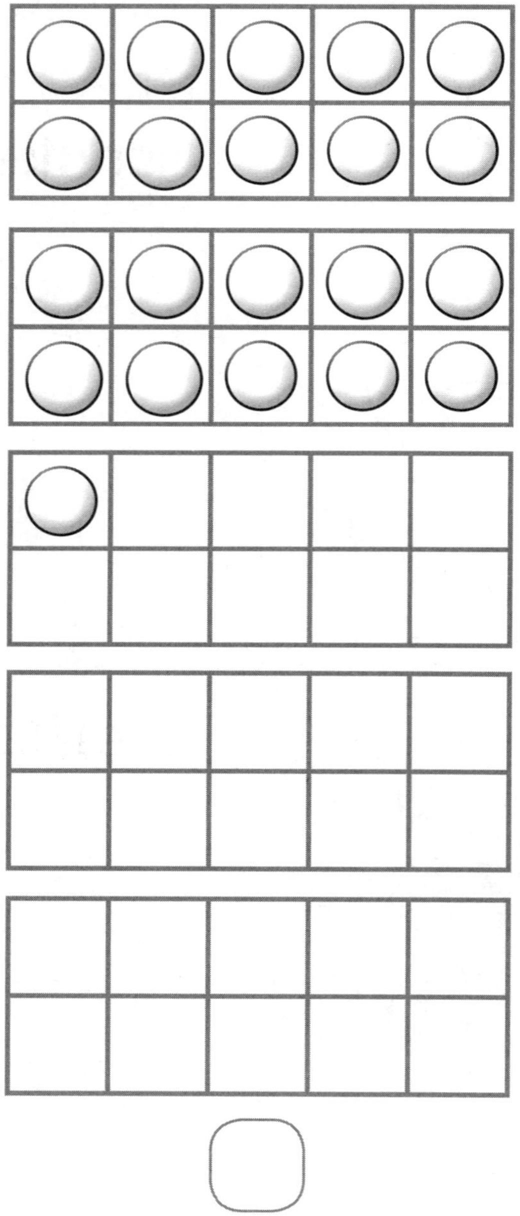

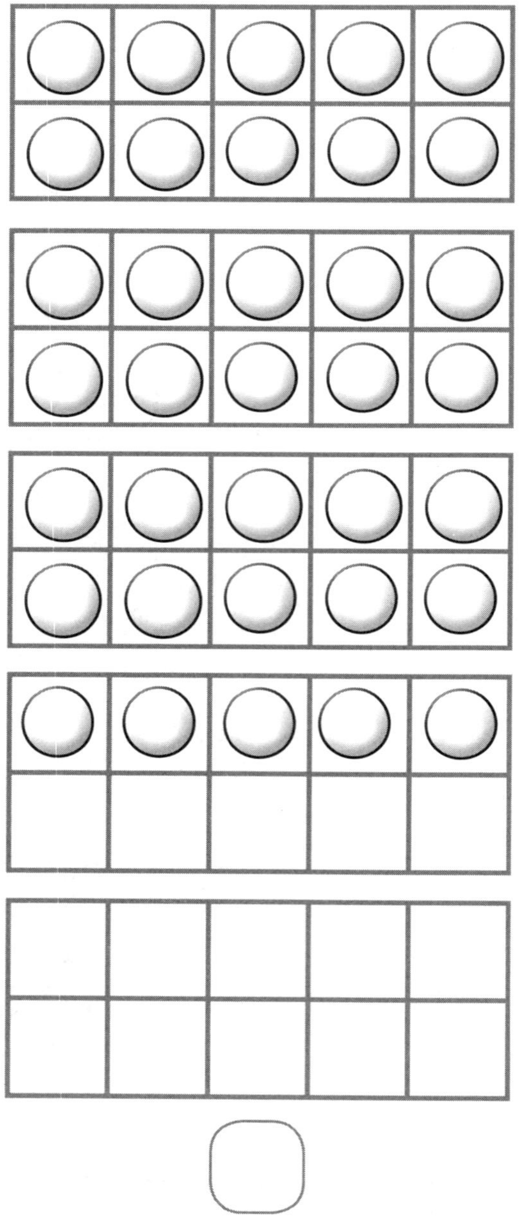

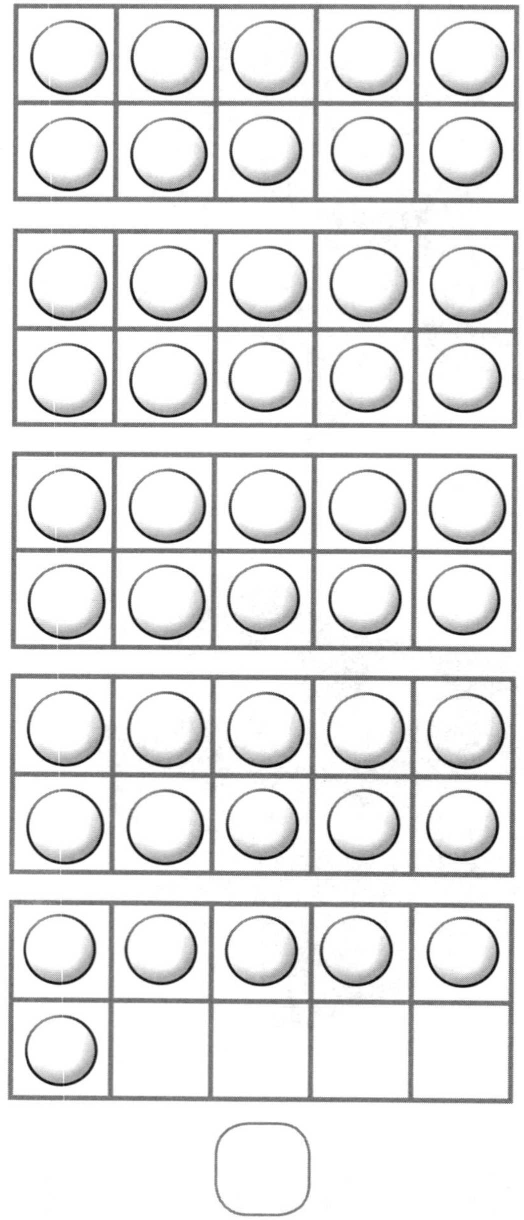

Objectives: Count to 50. Write numbers to 50.

Developmental Writing

Learning to Know

Trace the words.

square mangoes small

milk short mom

Draw a picture for each word.

Objective: Trace words with s and *m*.

What is your favorite activity?

Artistic Expression and Appreciation

Learning to Be

Complete the sentence.

I like ______________________.

Objective: Express which their favorite activities are.

Self-care

Learning to Do

Find a magazine. Cut out and paste the things you bring to school.

Objective: Reflect on how to take care of personal belongings at school.

Color the words with /d/.

Objectives: Practice the /d/ sound

Mathematical Thinking

Learning to Know

- **Complete the sequence. Color using blue, yellow, and green in a pattern.**

1						7			10
11		13	14	15		17	18		
21	22		24	25		27	28	29	30
	32	33		35	36	37		39	
41	42	43		45	46		48	49	50

Objectives: Identify missing numbers to 50. Extend color patterns.

Trace.

Developmental Writing
Learning to Know

D D D D D D D D

d d d d d d d d d

Look and write the words.

dad

dog

Objectives: Trace letters *D* and *d*.

Artistic Expression and Appreciation

Learning to Be

Fingerpaint two flowers.

Circle your answer.

Flowers smell good / bad.

Objectives: Use different painting techniques to represent objects. Describe a smell.

Self-care

Learning to Do

Match the pictures with the nose if the objects have a smell.

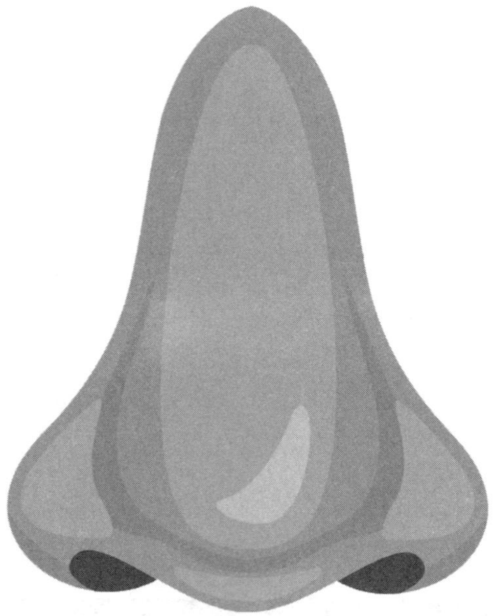

Objectives: Learn about the senses: smell.

Trace and draw.

lollipop

Lily

lamp

lion

Objectives: Practice the /l/ sound.

Mathematical Thinking

Learning to Know

Count and color. Write the number of shapes.

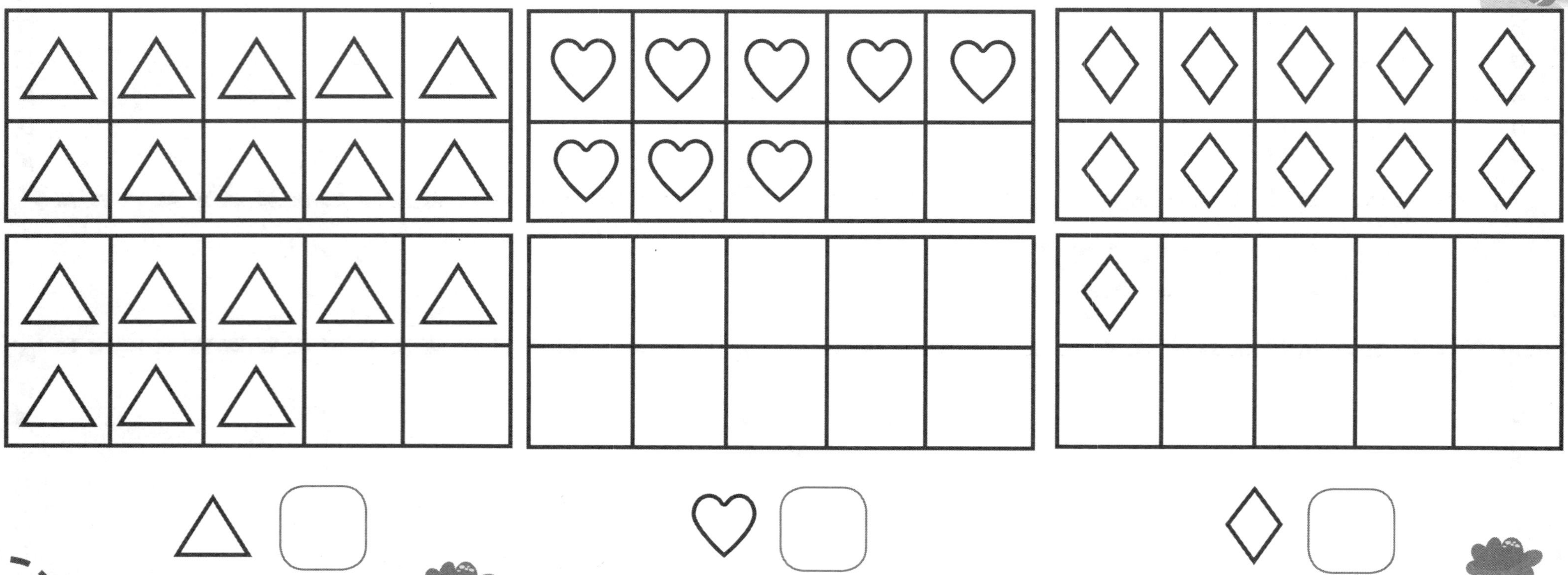

Objectives: Represent a number of items on ten-frames. Identify shapes.

Trace.

Developmental Writing

Learning to Know

hot hot

cold cold

Look and trace the correct word.

hot cold

hot cold

hot cold

hot cold

Objectives: Trace the letters *t* and *d*.

Mix and paint.

Artistic Expression and Appreciation

Learning to Be

red + yellow

red + blue

red + green

Objectives: Mix colors to make different colors.

Self-care

Learning to Do

What do these foods taste like? Match the pictures.

Objectives: Learn about senses: taste.

Phonemic Awareness

Learning to Know

- **Trace.**

Tom has a toy tiger.

- **Draw a picture about Tom.**

Objectives: Practice /t/ sound.

- **Trace the symmetry lines.**
  Color the objects.

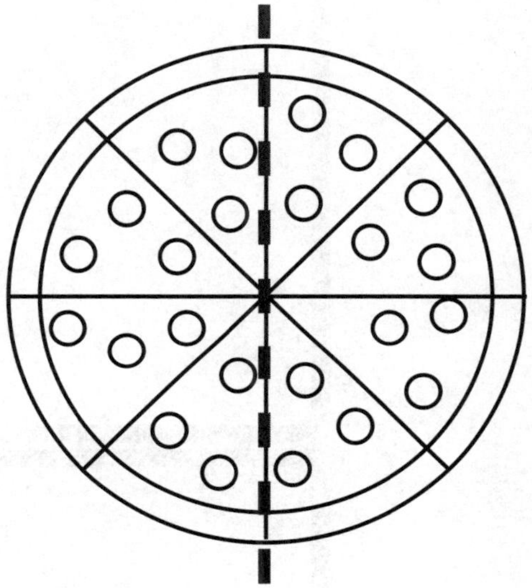

- **Find something symmetrical and paste it.**

Objectives: Identify symmetry lines.

Trace. Draw the musical instruments.

Developmental Writing

Learning to Know

drum

cymbal

triangle

tambourine

Read and circle the correct word.

The  is loud / quiet.

Objectives: Read and trace words related to musical instruments.

Use yarn to make spaghetti. Paste and draw.

Artistic Expression and Appreciation

Learning to Be

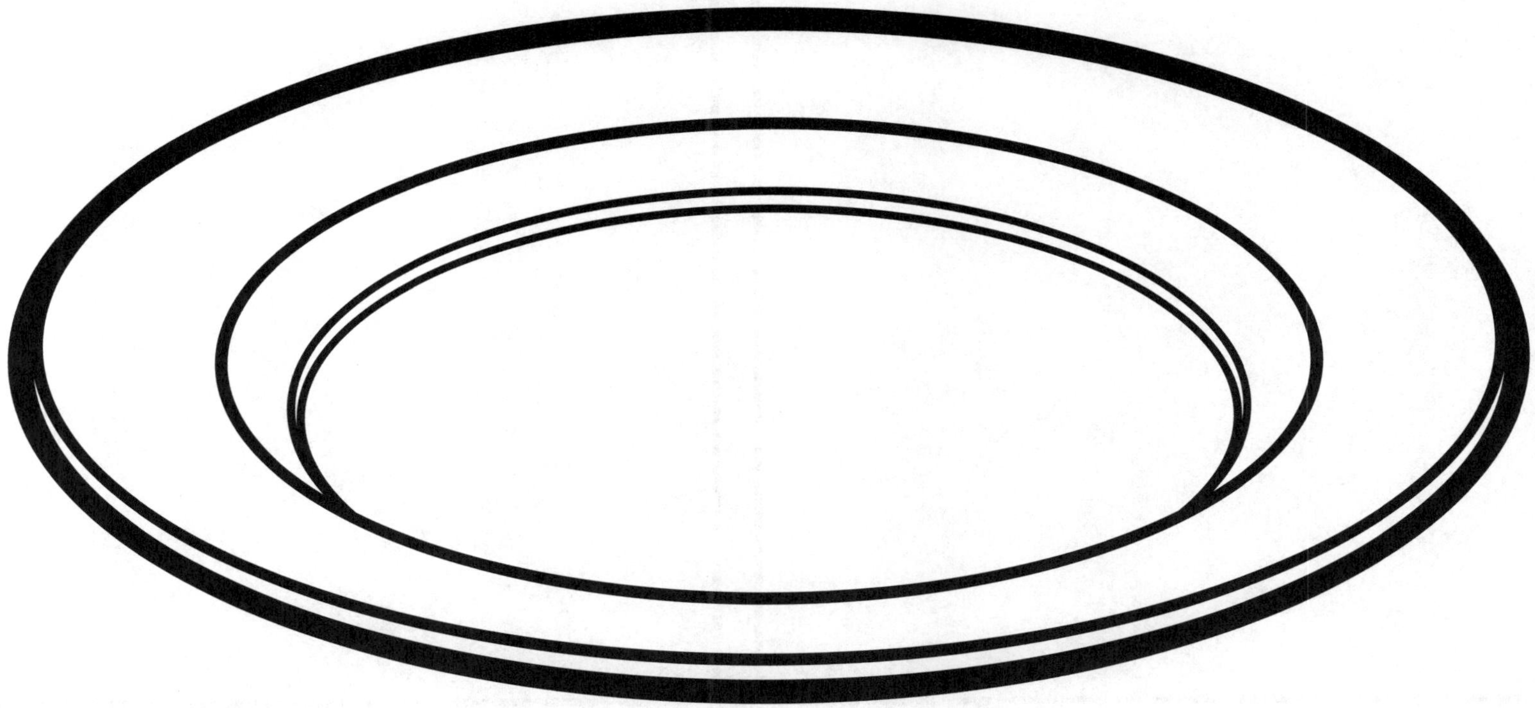

Objectives: Develop fine motor skills.

Complete the sentences and draw.

Self-care

Learning to Do

I can ____.

I can't ____.

Objectives: Learn to face challenges and develop strategies to overcome them.

Phonemic Awareness

Learning to Know

Complete the words. Match them with the pictures.

___ree

___uck

___ook

Objectives: Identify the /d/, /l/, and /t/ sounds.

Write the month, the day, and the number.

Mathematical Thinking

Learning to Know

Month: ______________________

Yesterday was...	Today is...	Tomorrow will be...

Write the complete the date.

Today is ______________________

Objectives: Write the day and the date.

Trace.

Developmental Writing

Learning to Know

hard soft warm

Complete the words.

ar   of   w

Objectives: Trace words related to touch.

Artistic Expression and Appreciation

Learning to Be

Paste a picture of something you like to do with each sense.

sight

smell

hearing

touch

taste

Objectives: Express what they like to do with their senses.

Physical Development and Health

Learning to Do

Follow the lines from the pictures to the instructions.

Taste candy!

Look at a book!

Touch the chair!

Objectives: Follow instructions related to the senses.

Look and complete. Color.

Phonemic Awareness

Learning to Know

____ueen

____uestion

Objectives: Identify the /q/ sound.

Complete and create a color pattern.

Mathematical Thinking
Learning to Know

blue - green - blue - yellow

1	2	3	4	5		7		9	
11		13		15		17		19	
21		23		25		27		29	

Count by 2's and write.

2 – 4 – ◯ – ◯ – ◯ – ◯ – ◯ – ◯

20 – 22 – ◯ – ◯ – ◯ – ◯ – ◯ – ◯

Objectives: Extend a color pattern. Count by 2's to 30.

Trace and draw.

Developmental Writing

Learning to Know

My Family

Mom

Dad

Grandma

Grandpa

Objectives: Write words for family members

Draw, paint, and decorate.

Artistic Expression and Appreciation

Learning to Be

Mom and Dad

Self-care

Learning to Be

Draw the generous thing to do.

Objectives: Learn to be cooperative, respectful, honest, and tolerant.

Trace.

Phonemic Awareness

Learning to Know

Z z Z z Z z Z z Z z Z

Read and draw.

A zebra in the zoo.

Complete the patterns. Color.

Mathematical Thinking

Learning to Know

Objectives: Extend complex patterns.

Circle the correct word.

short tall

old young

Trace and complete.

short

old

Objectives: Identify characteristics of people related to size and age.

Fingerpaint the hair.

Artistic Expression and Appreciation

Learning to Be

brown

black

blond

my hair

Objectives: Say the differences in people according to hair color.

Check the chores you did this week. ✔

Self-care

Learning to Be

	Monday	Tuesday	Wednesday	Thursday	Friday
	○	○	○	○	○
	○	○	○	○	○
	○	○	○	○	○
	○	○	○	○	○

Objectives: Talk about chores and responsibilities at home.

Trace and match.

six

box

xylophone

x-ray

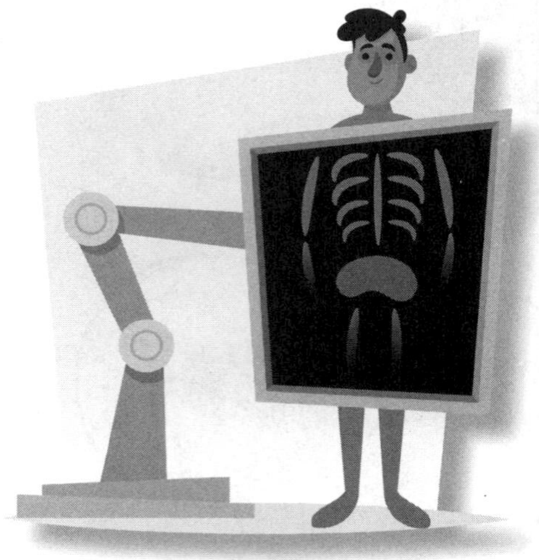

Objectives: Identify the sound of letter *x*.

Mathematical Thinking

Learning to Know

Look around your classroom, count, and color.

Objectives: Draw a simple picture graph.

Complete and draw.

Developmental Writing

Learning to Know

My ________________

looks after me.

I look after

________________.

Objectives: Talk about different kinds of families and their roles.

Draw a chore you do at home.

Artistic Expression and Appreciation

Learning to Be

Objectives: Talk about different responsibilities at home.

Self-care

Learning to Be

- **What do you like to do with your friends? Draw.**

- **Circle the correct word.**

My friends make me happy / sad.

Objectives: Be enthusiastic when spending time with other boys and girls.

Complete and color.

Phonemic Awareness

Learning to Know

ueen

ebra

bo

oo

si

uestion

Objectives: Review /z/, /x/, and /q/ sounds.

Think and circle.

Who is heavier?
Grandpa / The boy

Who is lighter?
Grandpa / The boy

Objectives: Identify language associated with measurement: *weight.*

Write and draw.

Developmental Writing

Learning to Know

What's your aunt's name?

What's your uncle's name?

What are your cousins' names?

Objectives: Ask and answer questions about family.

Find and color the utensils.

Artistic Expression and Appreciation

Learning to Be

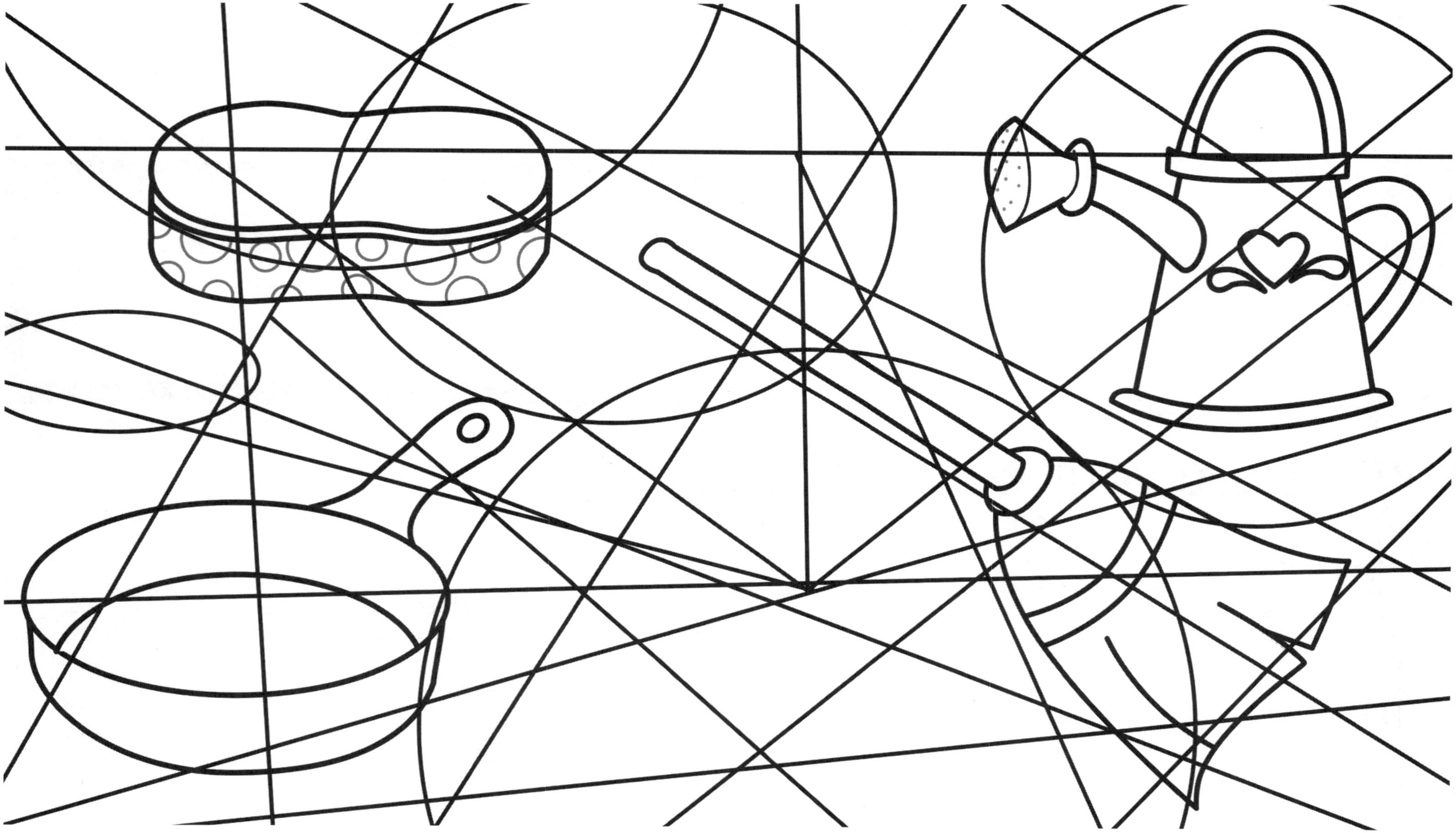

Objectives: Identify utensils that students can use at home.

Cross out the unkind actions. X

Self-care

Learning to Be

Circle.

I am kind / unkind.

Objectives: Be kind when spending time with other boys and girls.

Trace.

P p

Draw.

purple	pail	pink

Objectives: Identify the /p/ sound.

Count, trace, and complete.

Mathematical Thinking
Learning to Know

	42	43	44	45				49	50
51			54	55		57		59	
61				65	66	67		69	
	72					77			

Complete with the numbers before and after.

	45	

	66	

	72	

Objectives: Count to 80. Identify numbers that come before and after.

Trace. Read and complete the picture. Color.

Developmental Writing

Learning to Know

This is a crab.

Crabs have eight legs.

Crabs walk on the sand.

Objectives: Talk about animals on the beach.

Artistic Expression and Appreciation

Learning to Be

Color the pictures using watercolors. Trace the words.

sunny

cloudy

Objectives: Talk about different kinds of weather. Use different painting techniques.

Match and color.

swimsuit swimming trunks shorts

Draw your outfit on a sunny day.

Objectives: Express preferences about different types of clothes.

Trace.

P p P p P p

Complete the words.

__ail

__late

__ie

Objectives: Identify the /p/ sound.

Look and extend the patterns.

Mathematical Thinking

Learning to Know

A A B A A B A A B

A B A C A B A C A

A B B C A B B C A

Objectives: Extend more complex patterns.

Developmental Writing

Learning to Know

Color the shark with white chalk.

Trace.

This is a great white shark.

Great white sharks are very big.

Objectives: Talk about and describe sea animals.

Artistic Expression and Appreciation

Learning to Be

Make a turtle with a stone.

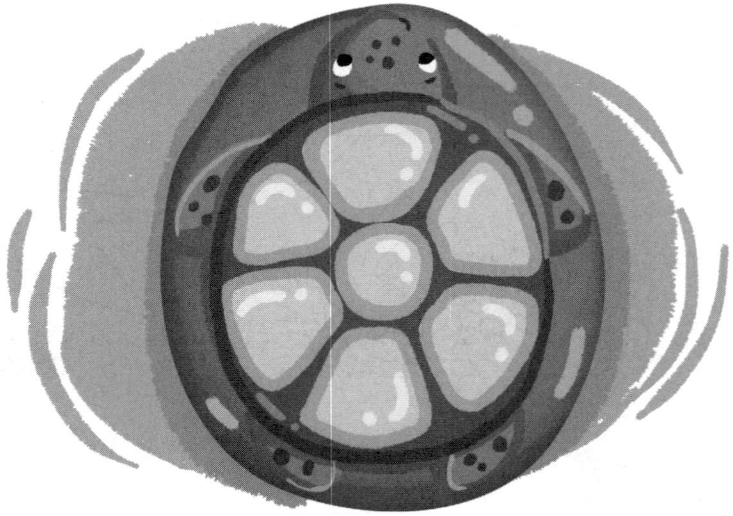

What color is your turtle? Write.

My turtle is ______________________.

Objectives: Talk about animals on the beach.
Use different painting techniques.

Put the pictures in the correct order.

Self-care

Learning to Be

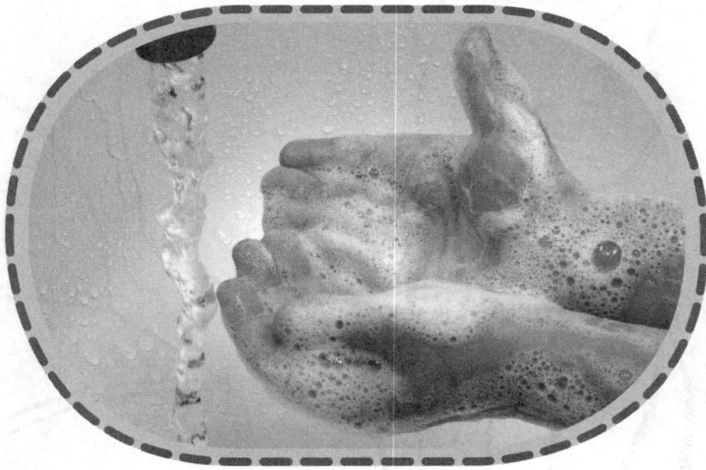

Check or cross out.

I keep my hands clean.

Objectives: Talk about how to keep hands clean.

Trace.

Phonemic Awareness

Learning to Know

crab cat cap

Write the words and color the pictures.

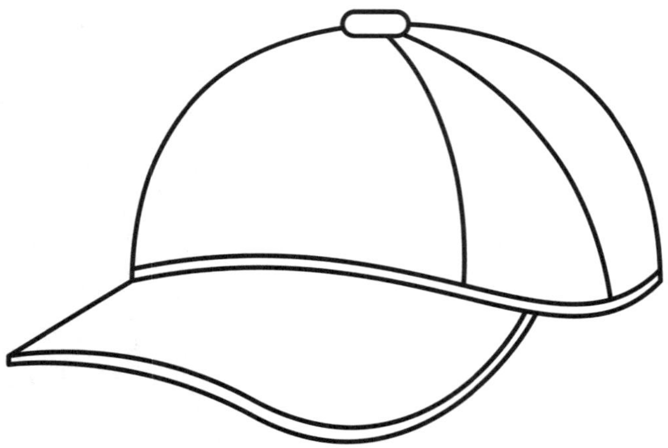

Objectives: Identify the /c/ sound.

Complete the symmetrical shapes.

Mathematical Thinking

Learning to Know

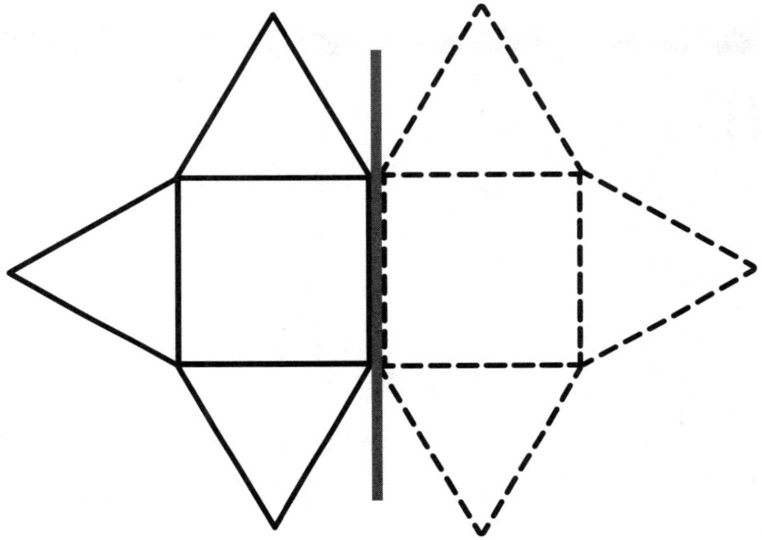

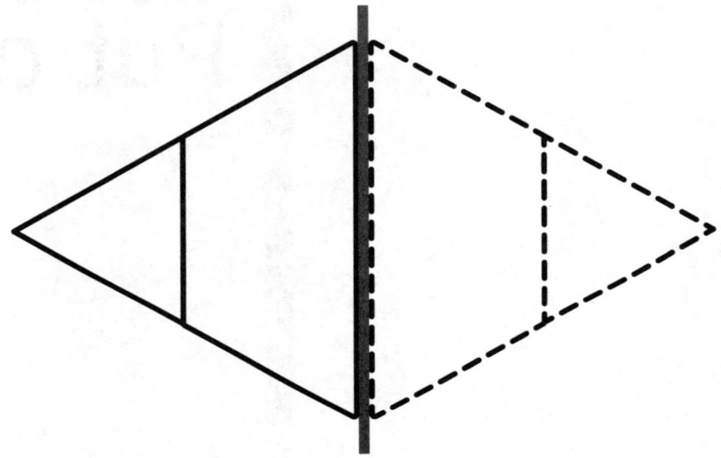

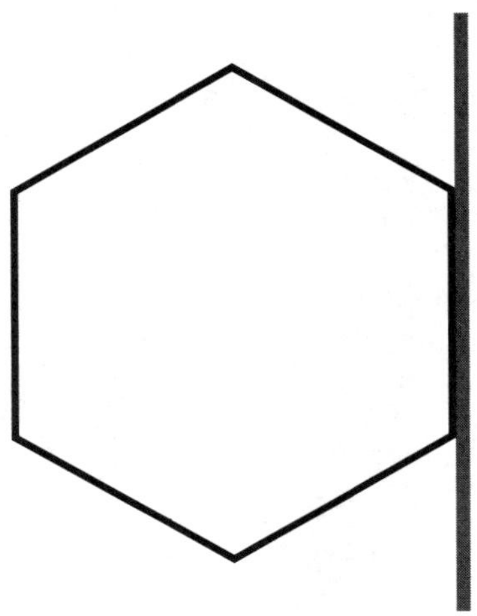

Objectives: Make simple symmetrical patterns using pattern blocks.

Trace, complete, and draw.

Developmental Writing

Learning to Know

It's cold.

Put on your ______.

It's hot.

Put on your ______.

Objectives: Talk about different kinds of weather and clothing.

Look and circle.

Artistic Expression and Appreciation
Learning to Be

My Closet

hot / cold

hot / cold

hot / cold

hot / cold

Paste pieces of paper on the clothes.

Objectives: Talk about different kinds of weather and clothing.

Self- care

Learning to Be

Draw how to protect the children from the weather.

Wear a hat.

Use sunscreen.

Use an umbrella.

Wear a sweater.

Objectives: Show how to take care of their bodies in different kinds of weather.

Trace the correct word.

cap shorts

fish crab

sun cloud

Circle the letter *c*.

Objectives: Identify the /c/ sound.

Look, think, and draw.

Mathematical Thinking

Learning to Know

Lighter	Heavier

Objectives: Identify language associated with mass.

Trace.

Developmental Writing

Learning to Know

in on under

Look and complete.

The crab is ______ the rock.

The turtle is ______ the water.

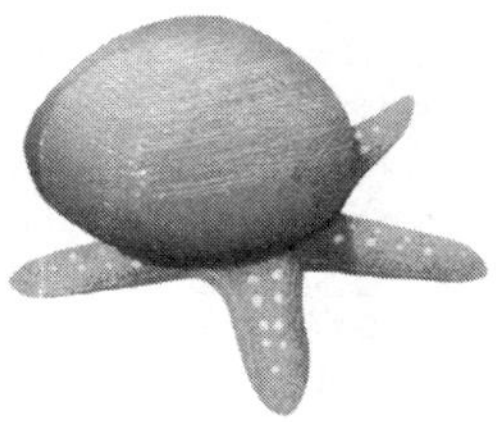

The starfish is ______ the rock.

Objectives: Talk about sea animals. Use prepositions of place.

Artistic Expression and Appreciation
Learning to Be

- **What's missing? Paste yarn to complete the octopus.**

Ollie The Octopus

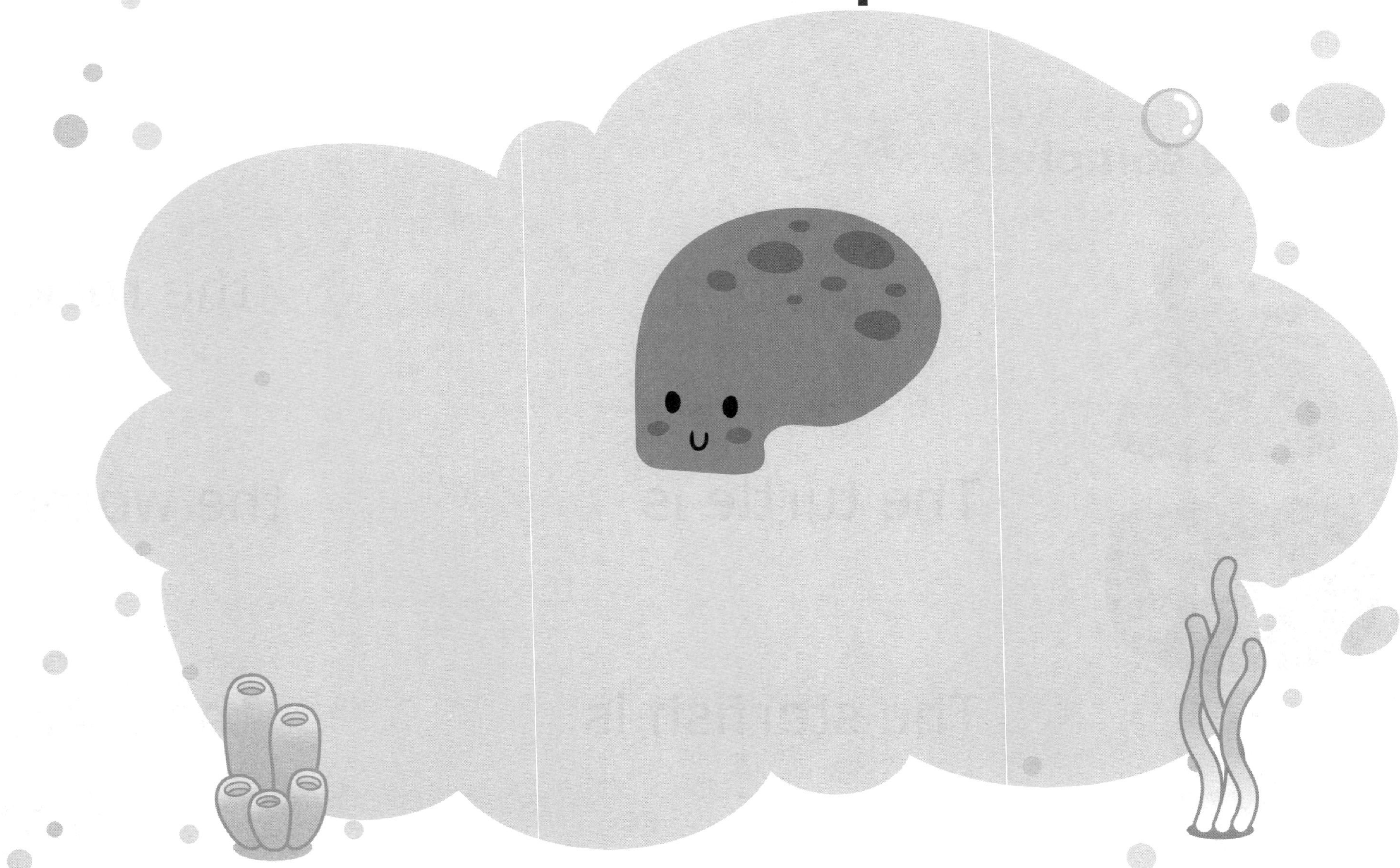

Objectives: Use different techniques to represent sea animals.

It's a cloudy day at the beach.
Draw yourself and a friend at the beach.

Self-care

Learning to Be

Objectives: Share experiences related to the beach.

Phonemic Awareness

Learning to Know

Trace and complete.

B b B b

Complete and draw.

__aby

__acon

__each

Objectives: identify the /b/ sound.

Look and draw the elements found at the beach.

Mathematical Thinking

Learning to Know

Objectives: Count objects in a simple bar graph.

Trace and match.

Developmental Writing

Learning to Know

shorts

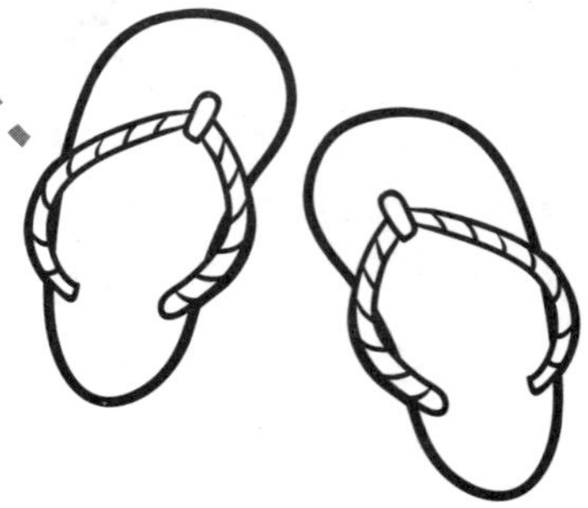

sandals

sweater

t-shirt

Objectives: Talk about clothing.

Artistic Expression and Appreciation
Learning to Be

- **Use the color code to discover the animals. Circle the answer.**

These are sharks / dolphins.

1 = gray 2 = blue 3 = orange 4 = yellow

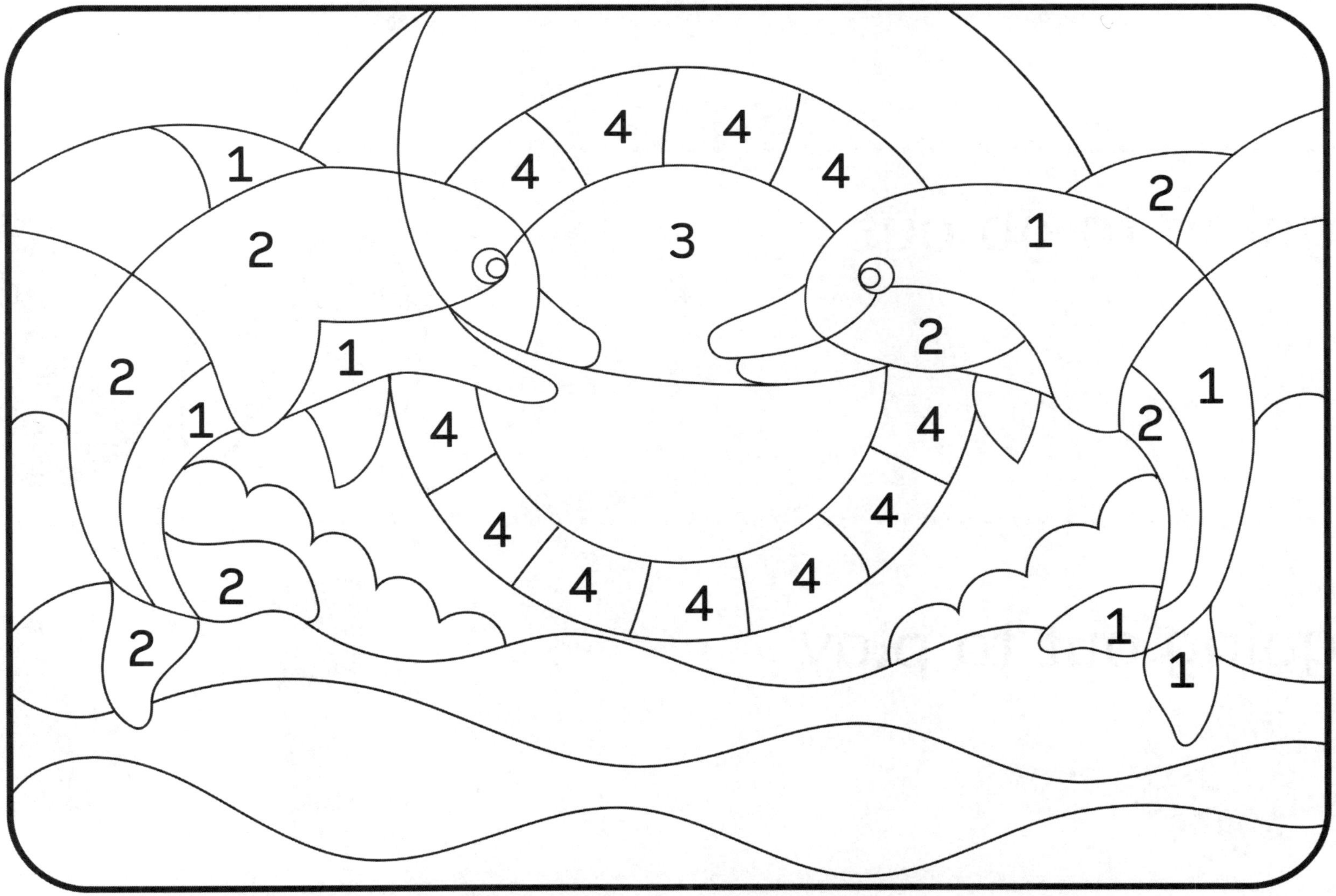

Objectives: Use different techniques to represent sea animals.

Read and circle what you need.

Self-care

Learning to Be

You're going to make a  .

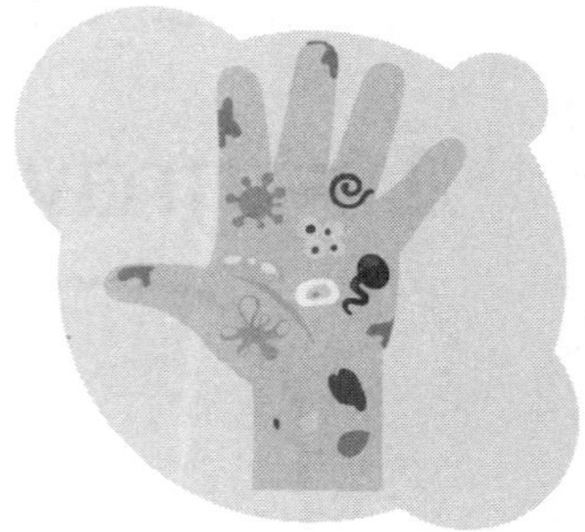

You're going to go out in the  .

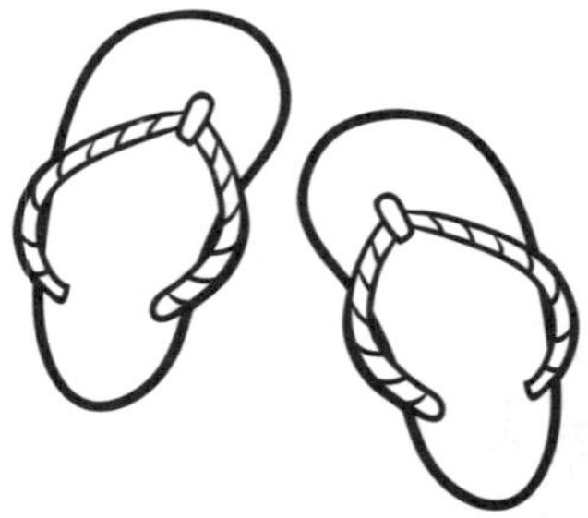

You're going out to play in the  .

Objectives: Learn about things you need.

Phonemic Awareness

Learning to Know

- Circle the words with the /b/ sound.
  Color the words with /c/ sound.

- Draw 2 words with /p/.

Objectives: Identify the /b/, /p/, and /c/ sounds.

Look and complete the ten-frames.

Mathematical Thinking

Learning to Know

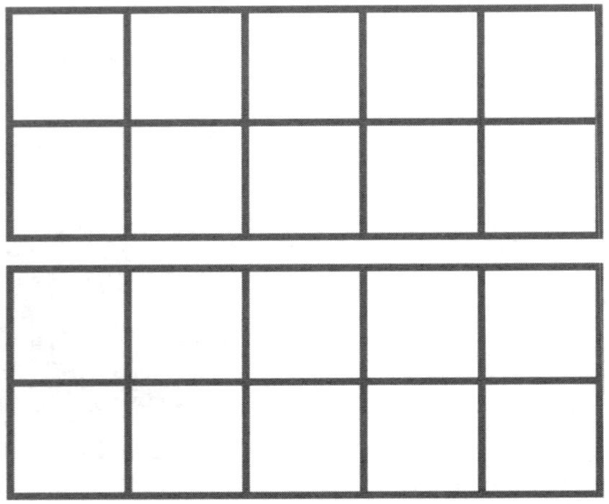

 =18

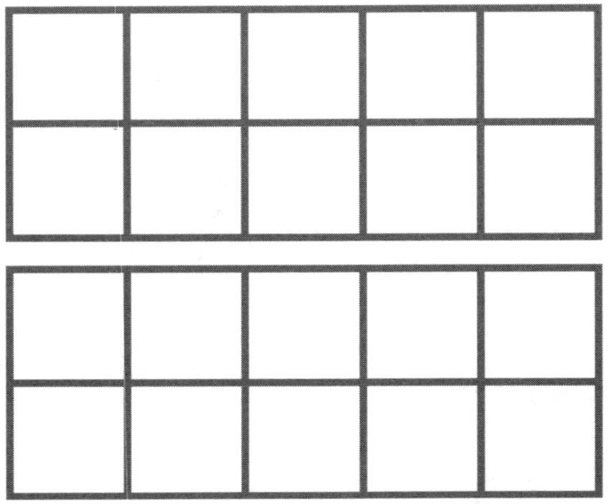

 =12

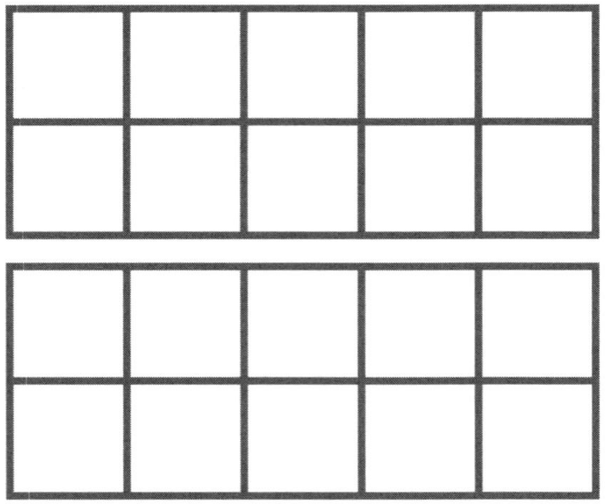

 =20

Objectives: Count and draw objects on a double ten-frame

Read, trace, and draw.

Developmental Writing

Learning to Know

Crispin is a crab.

Crispin lives under a rock.

Crispin has many friends.

Objectives: Talk about sea animals.

Draw your favorite sea animal. Write.

Artistic Expression and Appreciation

Learning to Be

My favorite sea animal is the ____________________

Objectives: Use different techniques to represent sea animals.

Read, choose, and check.

Self-care

Learning to Be

On a sunny day, I like to ...

On a rainy day, I like to ...

Objectives: Share experiences with others related to weather.

Phonemic Awareness

Learning to Know

Circle the correct word.

Neddy

Nicola

eight

nine

Trace.

N n N n N n N

Objectives: Identify the /n/ sound.

Mathematical Thinking

Learning to Know

Count, trace, and complete.

51	52	53	54	55		57		59	
		63	64	65		67		69	
71	72			75			78	79	
		83	84	85	86	87		89	
	92		94		96	97			

Count by 10's. Trace and complete.

10	20	30	40		60				

Objectives: Rote count to 100. Count by 10's.

Trace the words.

animals flowers trees people

Complete the sentences.

Animals live on the planet.

_______________ live on the planet.

Objectives: Learn about animals, plants, and habitats.

Draw a garden. Color it with markers.

Artistic Expression and Appreciation

Learning to Be

Objectives: Identify what plants and animals live in a garden.

Choose the right thing to do. Trace.

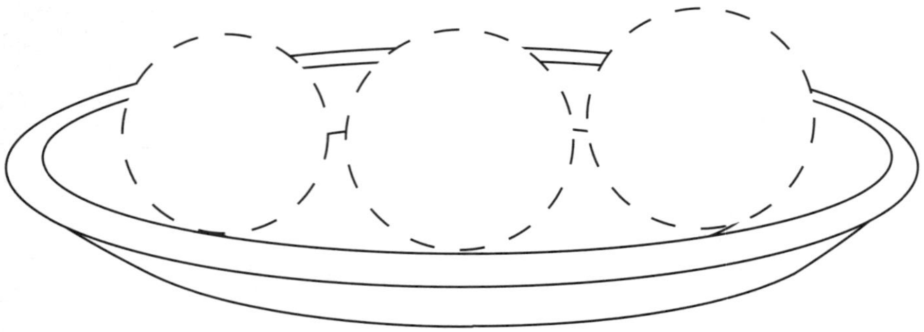

Eat turtle eggs. / Don't eat turtle eggs.

Cut down the trees. / Don't cut down trees.

Use plastic bags. / Don't use plastic bags.

Objectives: Identify how to help the environment.

Trace and complete.

F f F f F f

Complete the words.

___lamingo

___rog

___lower

Objectives: Identify the /f/ sound.

Complete the pattern. Write the letters.

Mathematical Thinking

Learning to Know

A A B C A A B C A A B C

A B A A B A B A A B A B

A B C D A B C D A B C D

Objectives: Extend more complex patterns.

Trace and match.

Developmental Writing

Learning to Know

Polar bears live
in the Arctic.

Monkeys live
in the jungle.

Camels live
in the desert.

Objectives: Identify the different habitats for animals and plants.

Exploration and Knowing of the World

Learning to Do

Check the correct actions. Cross out the incorrect actions. ✓ X

Objectives: Learn about keeping their environment clean.

Self-care

Learning to Be

Draw what makes you happy and sad when you go to the park.

Happy

Sad

Phonemic Awareness

Learning to Know

Trace and complete.

R r R r R r

Circle the /r/ sound. Color.

rabbit

river

rose

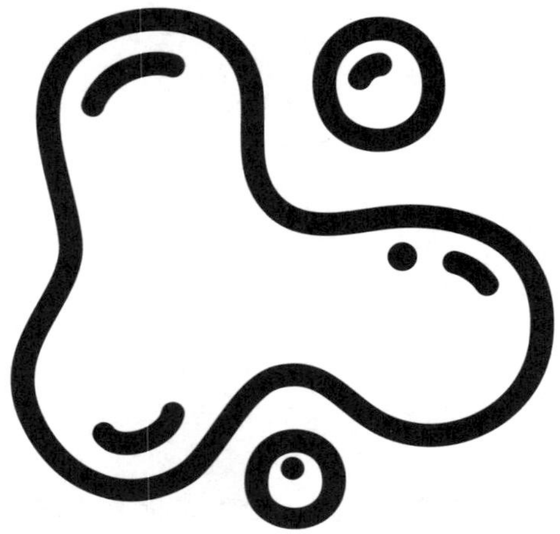

red

Objectives: Identify the /r/ sound.

Mathematical Thinking
Learning to Know

Draw the animals in the correct box.

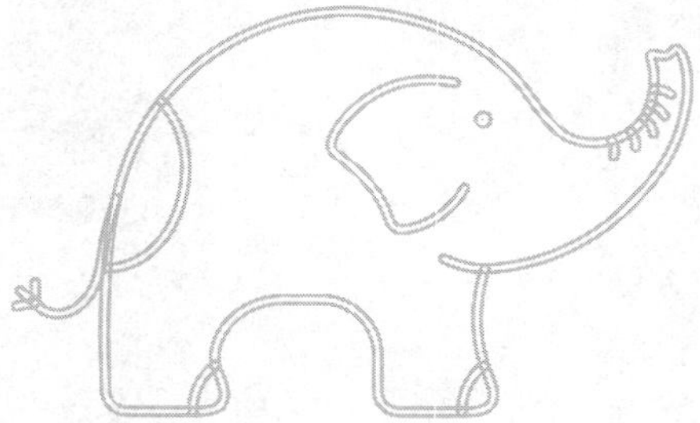

Heavier	Ligther

Objectives: Sort objects according to their nature.
Identifies language associated with mass.

Trace and match.

Developmental Writing

Learning to Know

Turn off the TV.

Don't litter.

Save water.

Objectives: Talk about how to take care of the environment.

Artistic Expression and Appreciation

Learning to Be

Match the instructions to the pictures. Make a pin of your favorite animal.

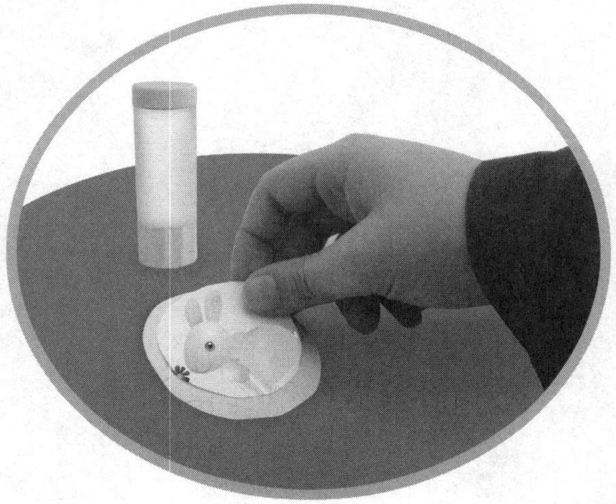

Glue a safety pin.

Cut out your favorite animal.

Wear your pin.

Paste your favorite animal.

Objectives: Represent their favorite animal using different techiniques.

Draw the clean solution.

Self-care

Learning to Be

Objectives: Express how problems in the environment make you feel.

Phonemic Awareness

Learning to Know

Trace and complete.

r n f

Draw pictures of words that begin with the sounds.

r	n	f

Objectives: Identify the /f/, /r/, and /n/ sounds.

- **Write the current month and year.**

Mathematical Thinking

Learning to Know

Month: ______________________ Year: ______________________

Monday	Tuesday	Wednesday	Thursday	Friday	Saturday	Sunday

- **Write the numbers in the calendar. Circle today's date.**

Objectives: Write the date. Write the missing numbers in a calendar.

Trace and match.

Draw a door on
the milk carton.

Cut the door out.

Paint and decorate
the milk carton.

Put some seeds inside.

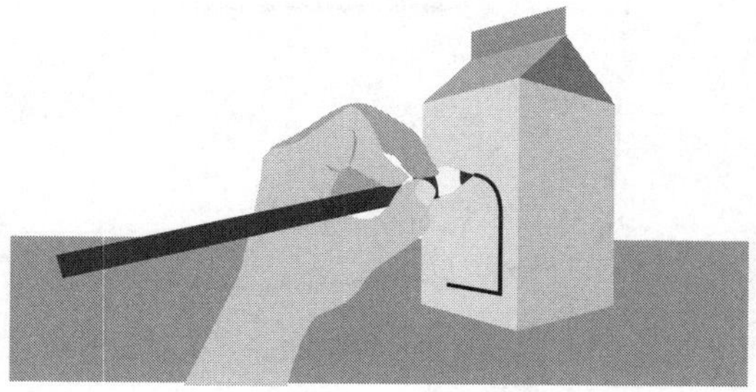

Objectives: Understand and follow instructions given by the teacher.

Artistic Expression and Appreciation

Learning to Be

Follow the code to color the recycling bins.

plastic = blue   paper = yellow   metal = gray

Objectives: Learn how to classify trash to recycle it.

Draw one thing you do to help the environment.

Objectives: Say how they can help the environment.

Phonemic Awareness

Learning to Know

- **Trace.**

Gg

- **Trace and match.**

Gertie is a gorilla.

Gertie likes grapes.

Objectives: Identify the /g/ sound.

Mathematical Thinking

Learning to Know

Count and complete.

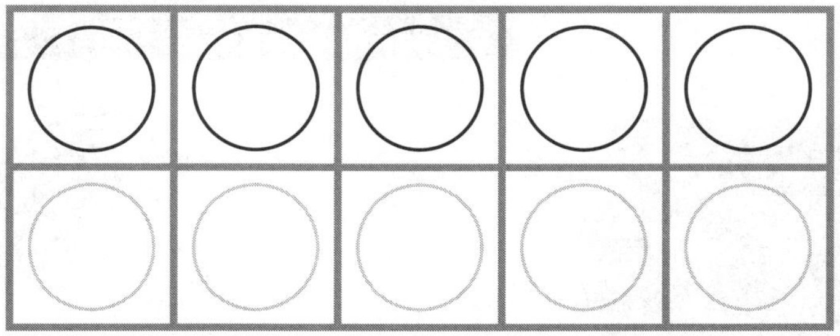

$5 + 5 = 10$

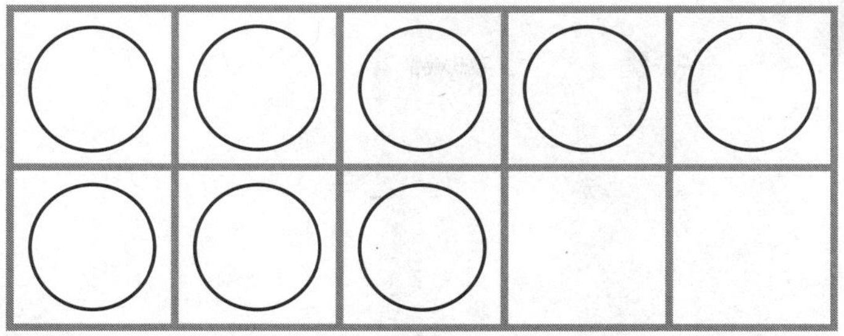

$8 + \square = 10$

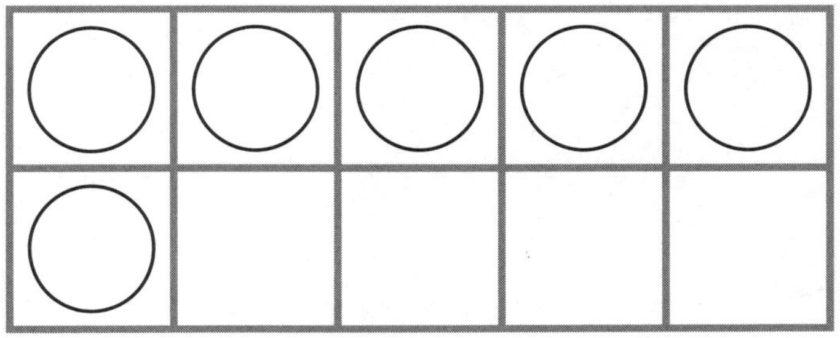

$\square + \square = 10$

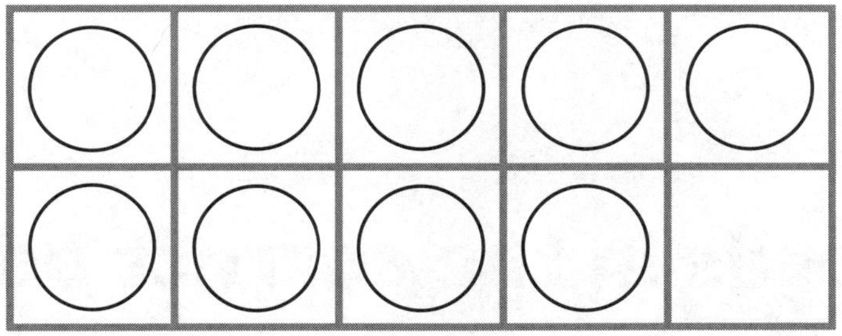

$\square + \square = 10$

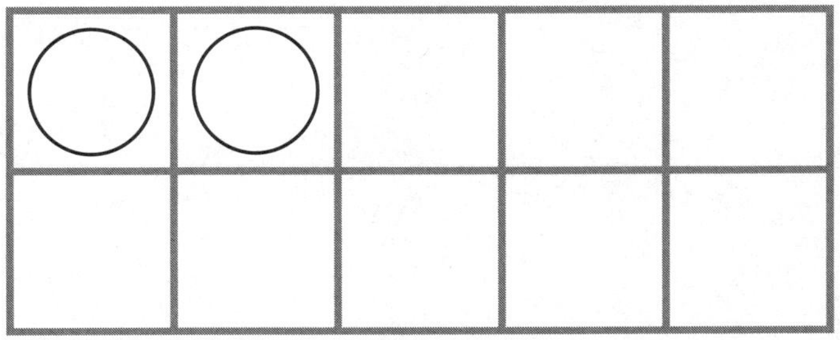

$\square + \square = 10$

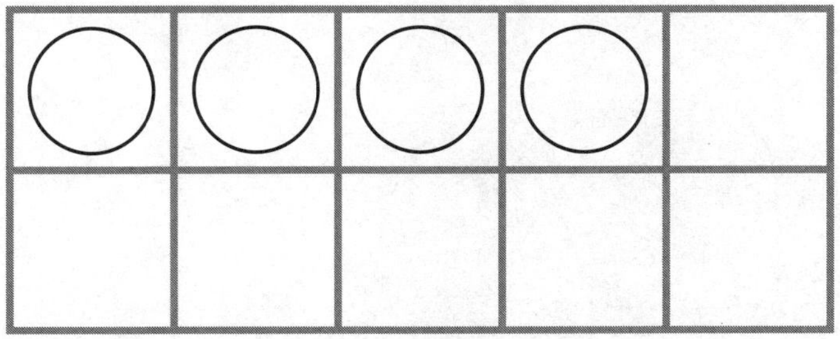

$\square + \square = 10$

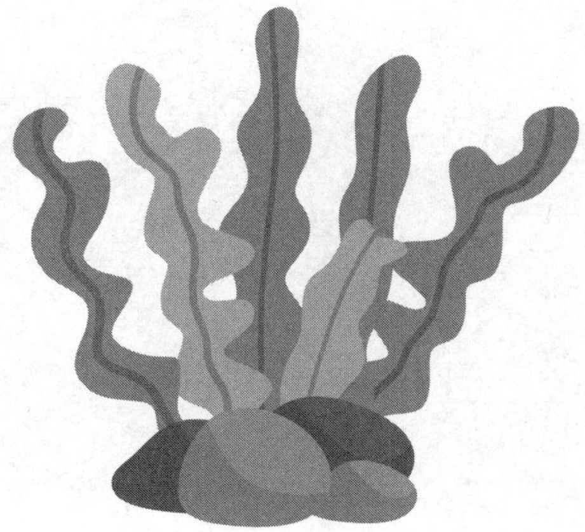

Objectives: Use double ten frames to add numbers.

Developmental Writing

Learning to Know

Trace.

apple water grapes ice cream

Write food words in the correct box.

Unhealthy	Healthy

Objectives: Learn key words for healthy habits.

Use small paper balls to match the correct way of sneezing.

Exploration and Knowing of the World
Learning to Do

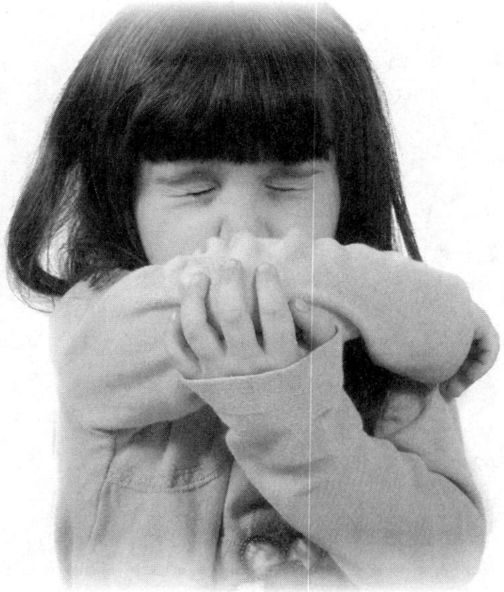

Objectives: Learn about healthy habits.

Color the proper thing to do.

Physical Development and Health

Learning to Be

Objectives: Identify who needs help and how they can help them. Identify solutions to health problems.

- **Follow the numbers to connect the dots. What is it? Write the word.**

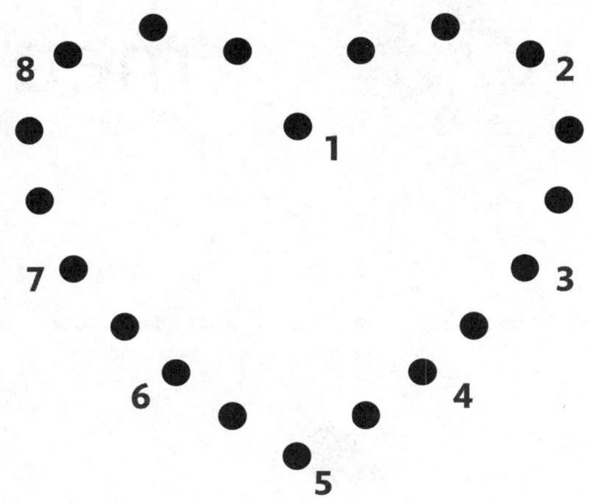

- **Draw 3 pictures of words beginning with /h/.**

Objectives: Identify the sound of letter *h*.

Mathematical Thinking

Learning to Know

Measure the objects with yarn.

My  measures this long.

My  measures this long.

My  measures this long.

Objectives: Measure objects using yarn.

Trace and match.
Complete the sentence.

Developmental Writing

Learning to Know

swim

run

hop

jump

I like to ____________________.

Objectives: Learn key words for healthy habits.

Paste yarn and color.
Paste paper balls and color.

Artistic Expression and Appreciation
Learning to Be

Exercise is good for you!

Objectives: Talk about staying healthy.

Physical Development and Health

Learning to Be

Complete with *happy* or *sad*.

When I  ,

I am feeling ______.

I need a  .

When I  ,

I am feeling ______.

I need to play all day.

Objectives: Talk about feelings.

- **Circle the odd one out in each line.**

Phonemic Awareness

Learning to Know

head

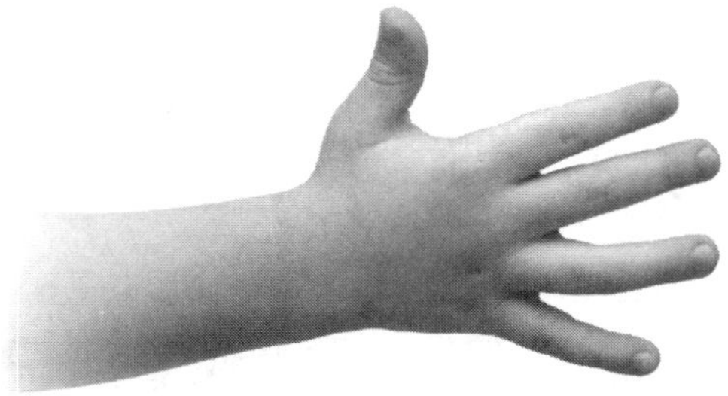

hand

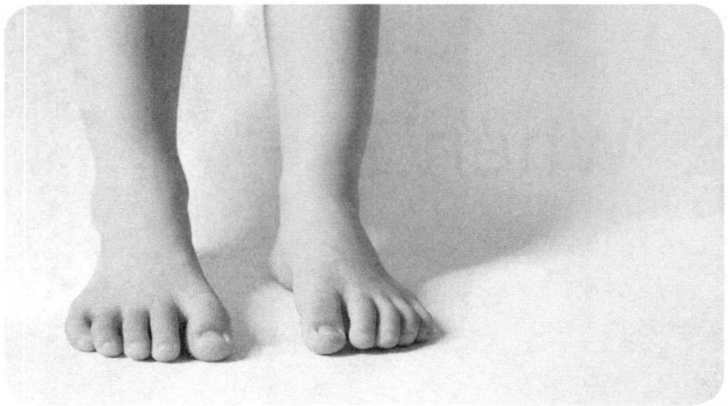

feet

grapes

flamingo

girl

Objectives: Identify the /g/ and /h/ sounds.

Mathematical Thinking

Learning to Know

Write the date.

Month: ____________________ Year: ______________

Sunday	Monday	Tuesday	Wednesday	Thursday	Friday	Saturday

Complete the calendar.

Objectives: Write missing numbers. Say the day and date.

● **Write the words next to the correct picture. Draw happy or sad.**

Developmental Writing

Learning to Know

cough | healthy | cold

Objectives: Use words related to feelings when they feel ill.

Artistic Expression and Appreciation

Learning to Be

What is it? Circle the correct word.

banana orange potato

Draw a cartoon of your favorite fruit or vegetable.

Objectives: Express likes and dislikes using different artistic techniques.

Physical Development and Health

Learning to Be

Find and color the food that is good for you.

Objectives: Identify food that is good or bad for you.

Phonemic Awareness
Learning to Know

Trace.

K k K k K k

Circle the /k/ sound in the words. Trace the pictures.

kitten

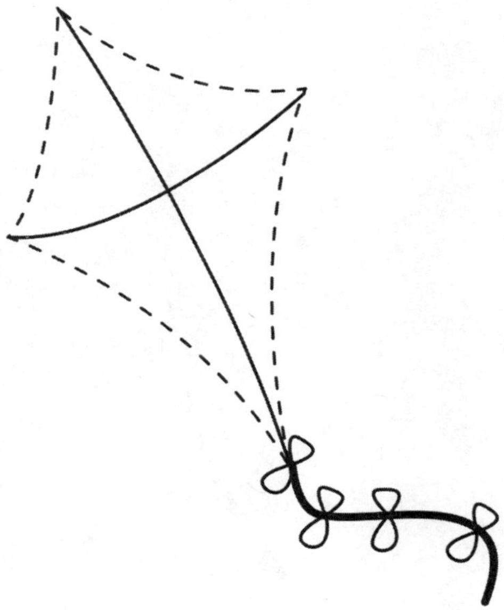

kite

kangaroo

Objectives: Identify the /k/ sound.

Complete the symmetrical figures.

Mathematical Thinking

Learning to Know

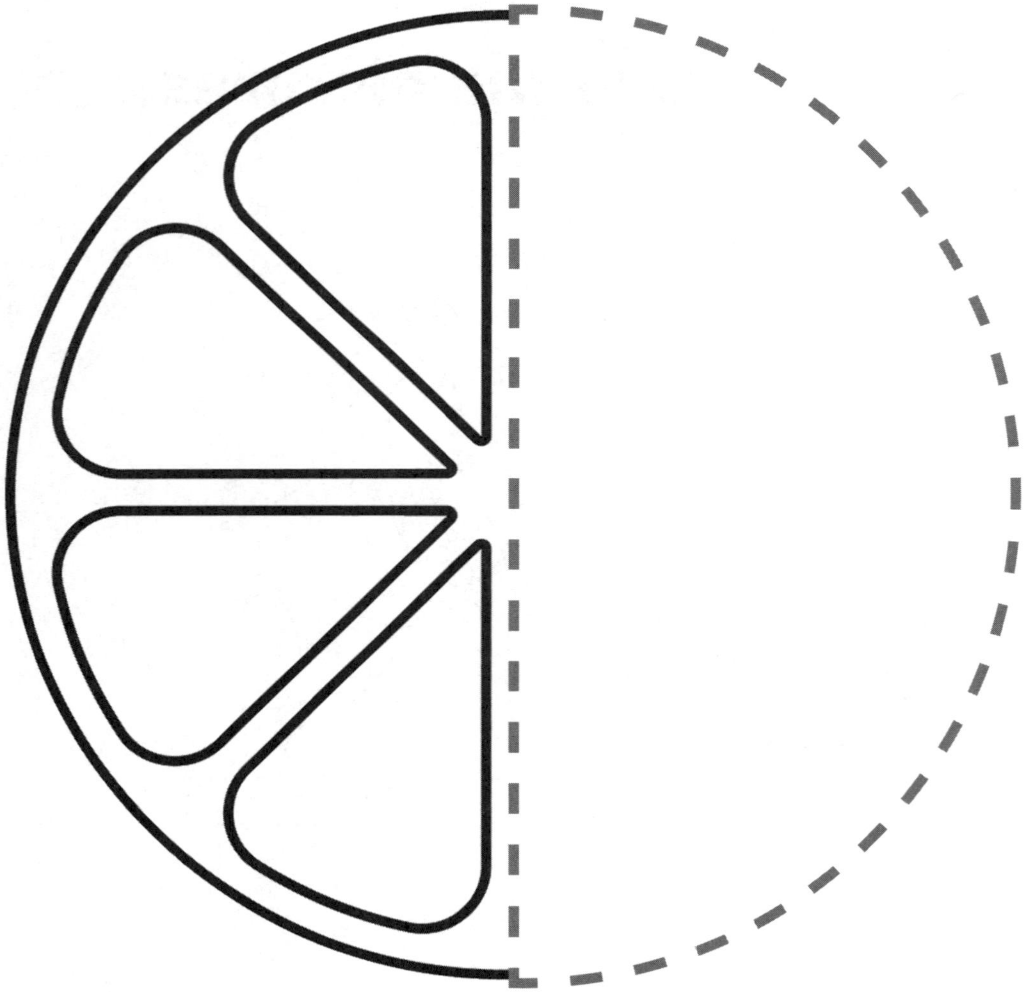

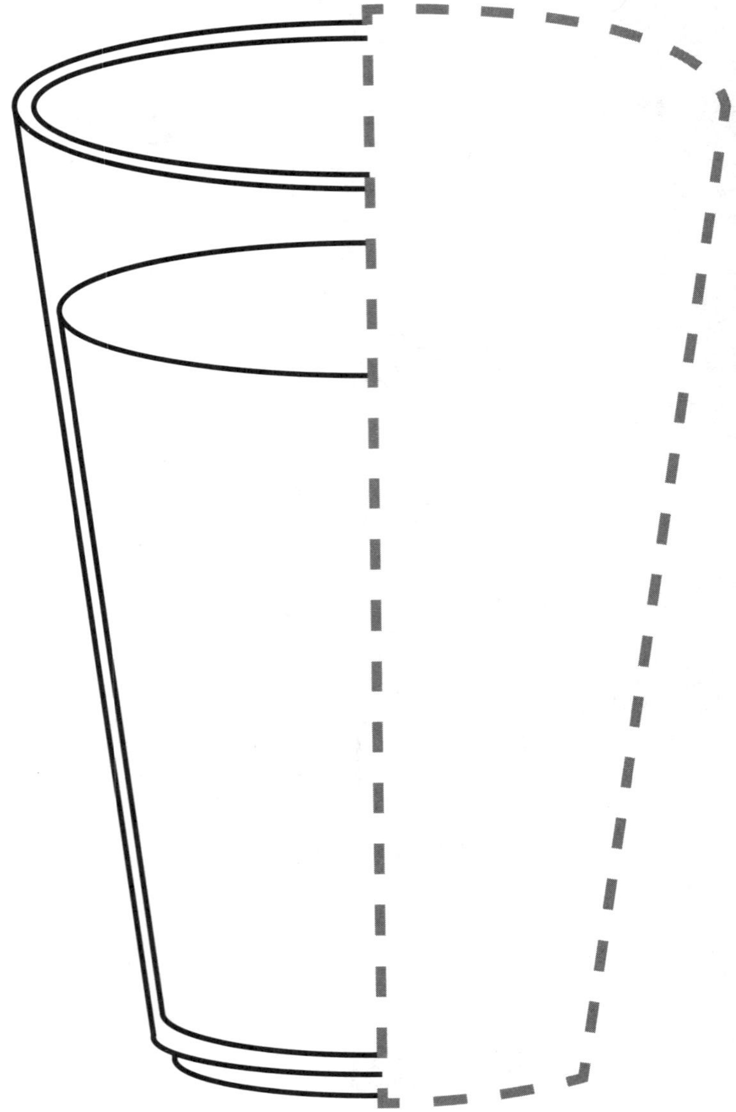

Objectives: Complete symmetrical figures.

Developmental Writing
Learning to Know

Trace and match.

How to Keep Your Teeth Clean

tooth

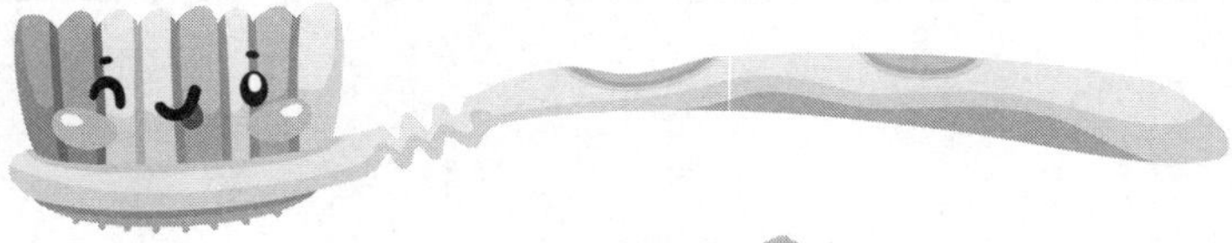

toothpaste

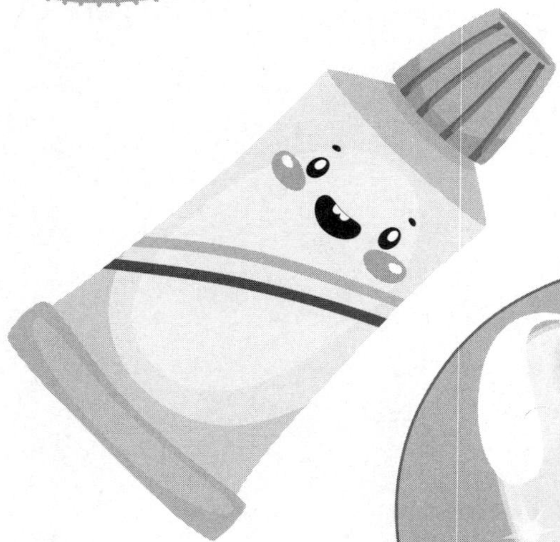

toothbrush

Complete the sentences.

This is a ________________.

Objectives: Describe a healthy habit.

Exploration and Knowing of the World

Learning to Do

- **Cut out from a magazine what you need to brush your teeth.**

- **Brush up and down. What happens? Circle.**

The teeth are clean / dirty.

Objectives: Understand the importance of brushing your teeth.

Match the pictures.

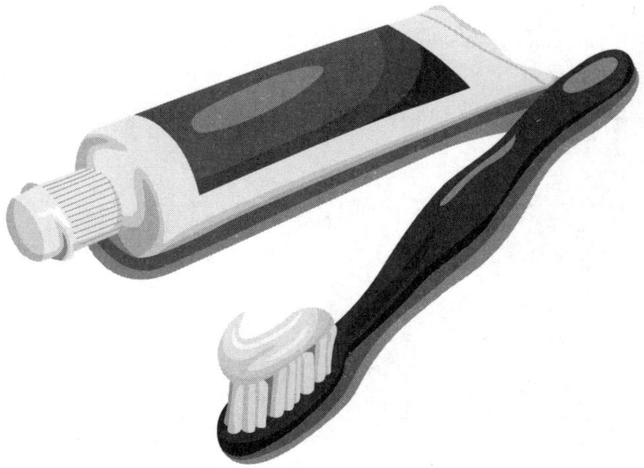

Check what you do before eating.

Objectives: Understand why it is important that we brush our teeth and wash our hands.

Phonemic Awareness

Learning to Know

Trace.

J j J j J j

Trace and draw.

juice

jello

jungle

Objectives: Identify the /j/ sound.

Extend the pattern. Trace the letters.

Mathematical Thinking

Learning to Know

A B A B C A B A B C A B

A B B B C C A B B B C C

A B C D A B A B C D A B

Objectives: Can extend more complex patterns.

Find the words and circle them.

Developmental Writing

Learning to Know

j	u	i	c	e	f
b	u	i	o	o	e
s	e	d	l	l	v
r	n	o	d	y	e
d	o	c	t	o	r

Complete the sentence.

I have a cold. I go to the ____________________.

Objectives: Talk about and describe health problems.

Draw the way out and color.

Watch Out!

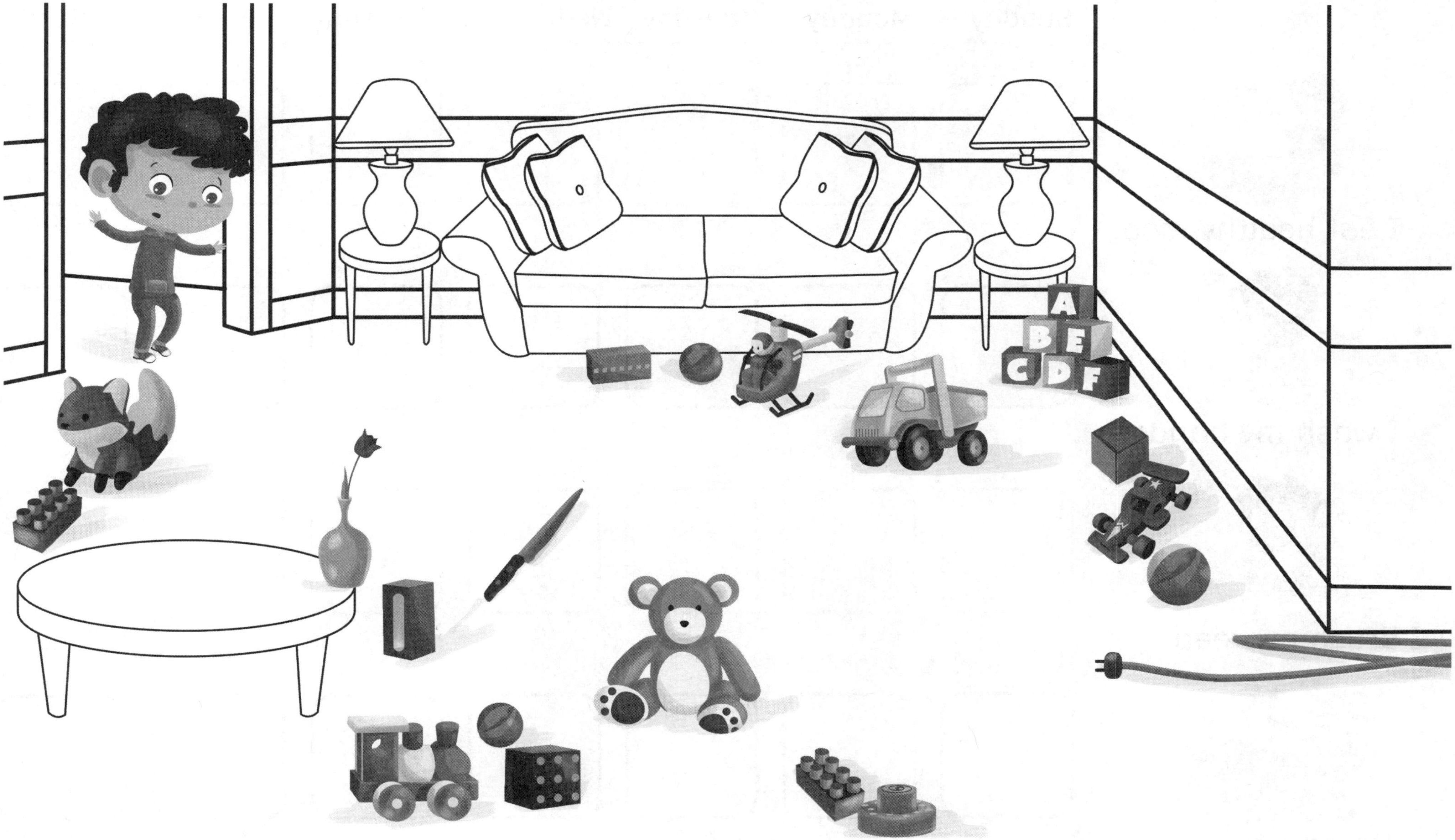

Check.

Self-Care

Learning to Be

My Healthy Habits Chart

	Sunday	Monday	Tuesday	Wednesday	Thursday	Friday	Saturday
 I eat healthy food.							
 I wash my hands.							
 I brush my teeth.							
 I exercise.							

Objectives: Learn healthy habits.

Phonemic Awareness

Learning to Know

Match the pictures to their beginning sound.

k

j

Draw a word with each sound.

Objectives: Identify the sound of letters *k* and *j*.

Mathematical Thinking

Learning to Know

Look and circle the differences.

Objectives: Talk about the location of things.

Trace.

Developmental Writing

Learning to Know

Games make you happy.

Games are fun!

Games are good for you.

Draw a picture of your favorite game.

I feel happy when I ...

Objectives: Use words related to feelings when they feel well.
Talk about healthy activities.

Make fruit stamps.

Artistic Expression and Appreciation

Learning to Be

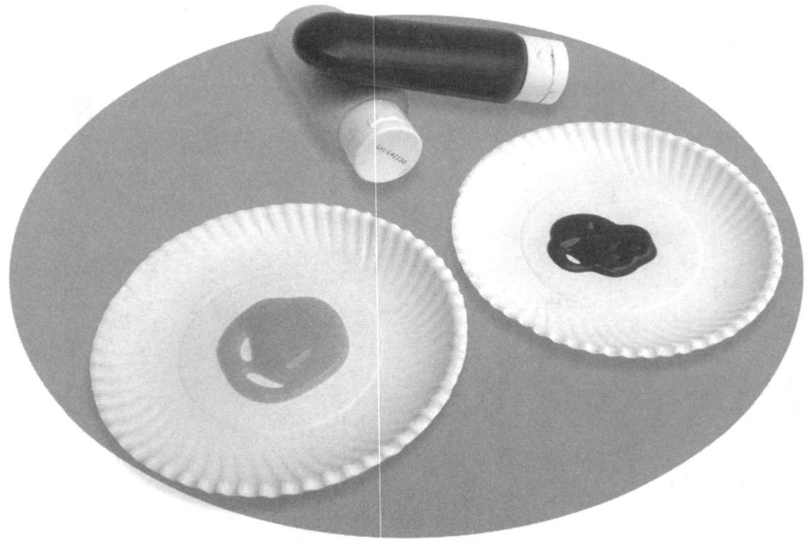

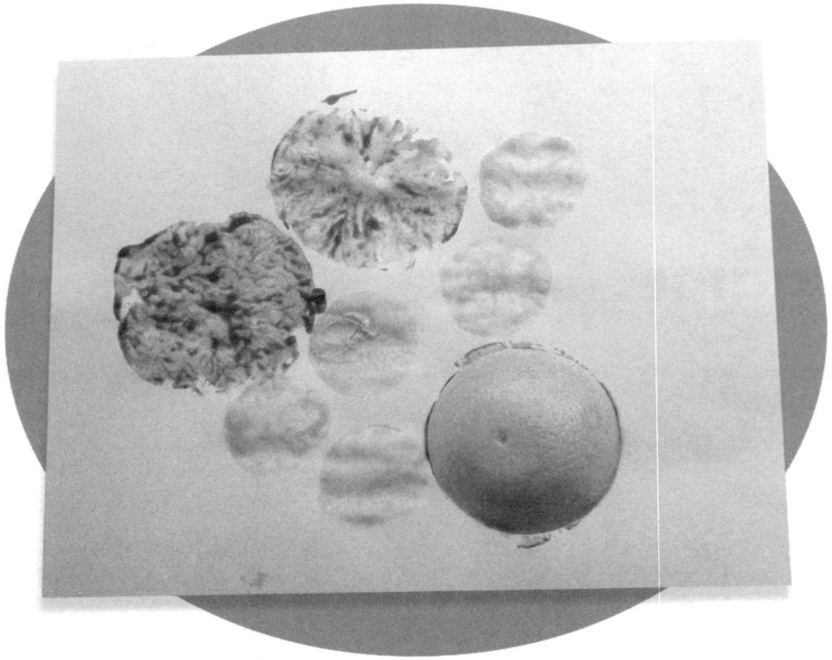

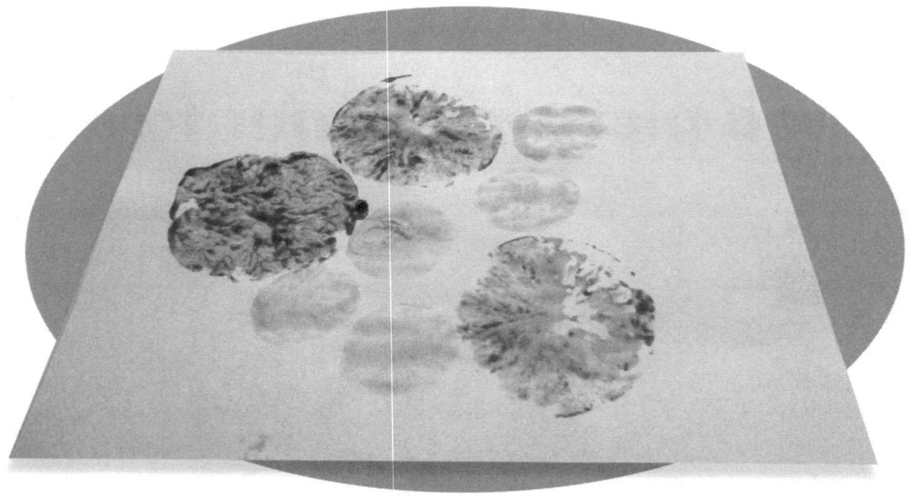

What fruit are you going to use? ____________

Objectives: Use different techniques with food to make a painting.

Physical Development and Health

Learning to Be

Draw 2 things that are good for you.

Draw 1 thing that is not good for you.

Objectives: Express what is good and bad for you.

Phonemic Awareness

Learning to Know

- **Trace and complete.**

W w W w

- **Complete the words. Draw a picture including the three words.**

__olf __oods __ater

Objectives: Identify the /*w*/ sound.

Mathematical Thinking

Learning to Know

Complete the chart.

1	2		4	5	6		8		10
	12								20
				25					
			44				48		50

Count by 10s. Use a blue colored pencil to write the numbers.

10 ☐ 30 ☐ 50

Objectives: Use a 100 chart to count by 2s, 10s, and 5s.

Trace and match.

Developmental Writing

Learning to Know

Polar bears live
in the Arctic.

They can swim.

They eat fish.

Objectives: Learn words for wild animals.

Artistic Expression and Appreciation

Learning to Be

Follow the steps to draw a polar bear. Paste cotton to make the fur.

Circle the things your dog needs.

Self-care

Learning to Be

Objectives: Learn to behave respectfully towards animals.

Phonemic Awareness

Learning to Know

Circle the words with the /v/ sound. Match them to the pictures.

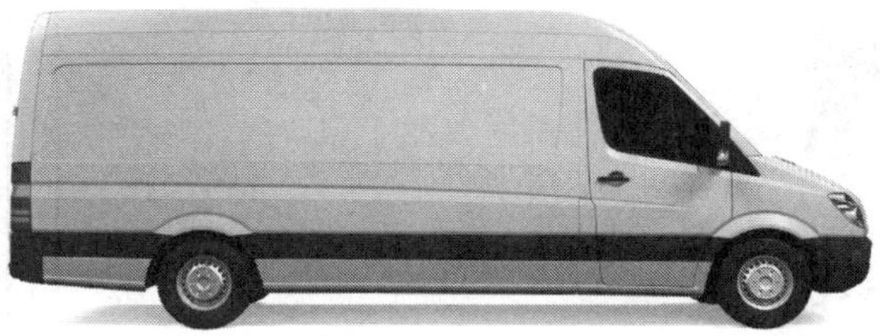

v	o	l	c	a	n	o
e	v	i	o	l	i	n
s	a	v	a	s	e	o
t	n	l	a	v	a	w

Objectives: Identify the /v/ sound.

Complete the graph. Draw the animals.

Mathematical Thinking

Learning to Know

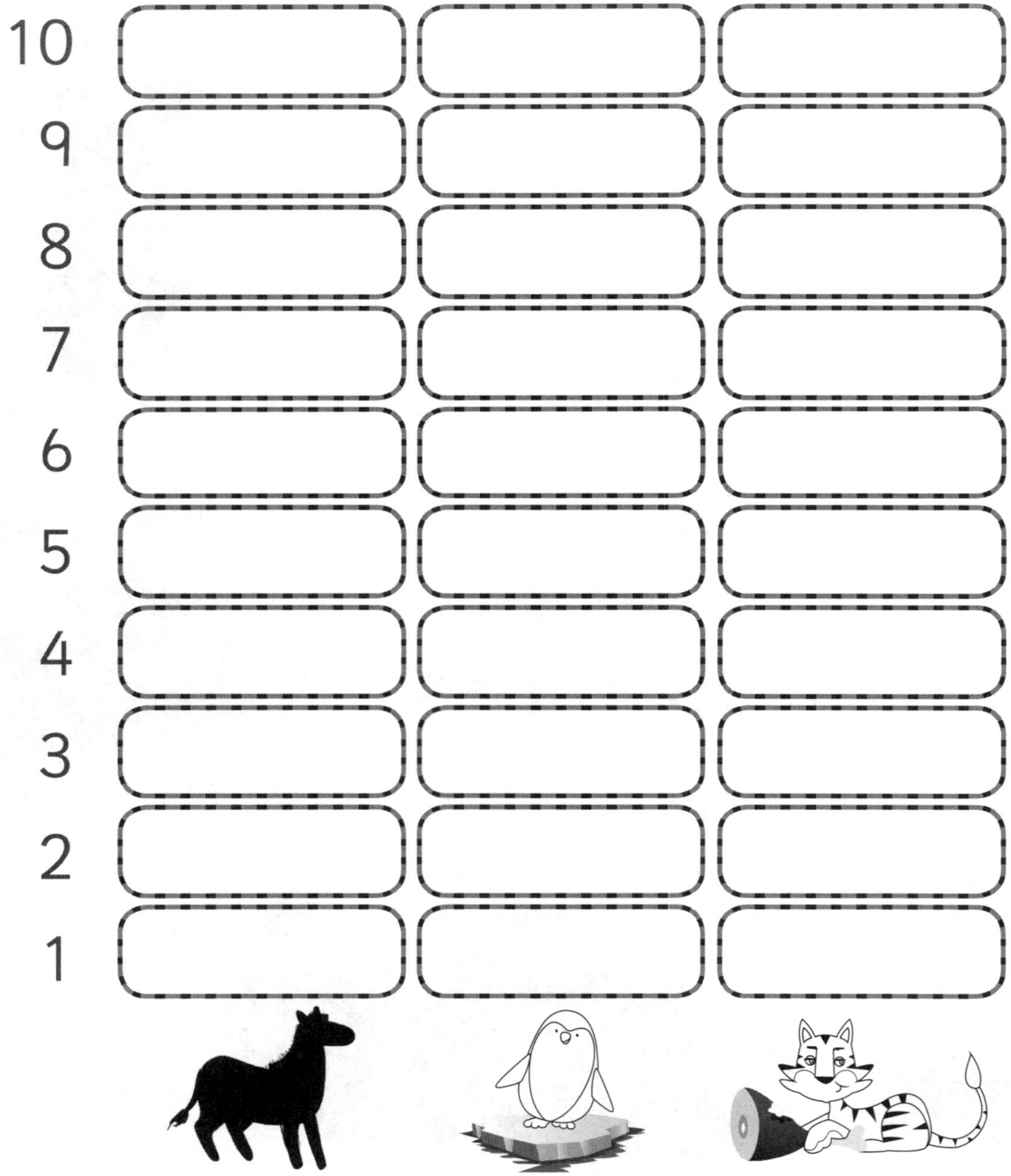

Objectives: Make a graph. Interpret results.

Trace the correct word to complete the sentences.

Developmental Writing

Learning to Know

A rhino is

big / small.

A chick is

big / small.

Objectives: Describe animals and their physical characteristics.

Match the animals with the tracks. Finger paint the tracks.

Exploration and Knowing of the World

Learning to Know

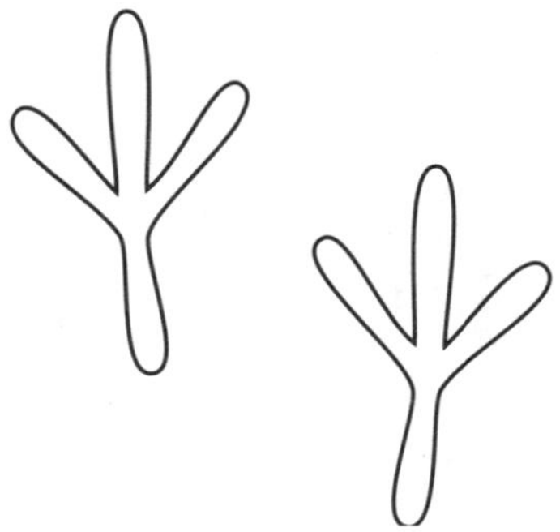

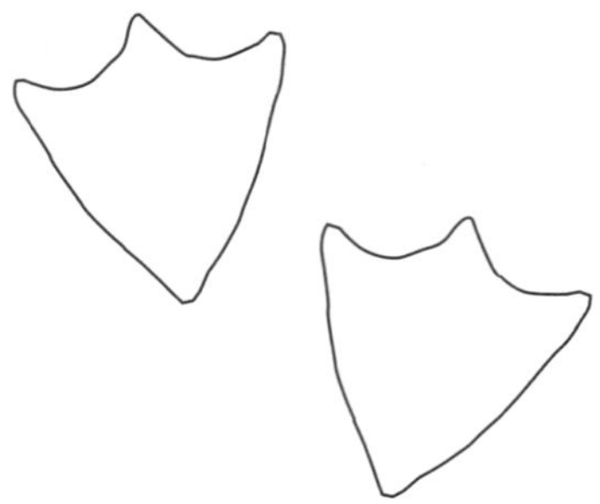

Objectives: Describe and talk about living things.

Number the pictures in the correct order.

Self-care

Learning to Be

What to Do If an Animal Bites You

Phonemic Awareness

Learning to Know

Trace and complete.

Y y Y y Y y

Trace and draw.

yellow flower

yellow yo-yo

Objectives: Identify the /y/ sound.

Circle the odd one out.

Mathematical Thinking

Learning to Know

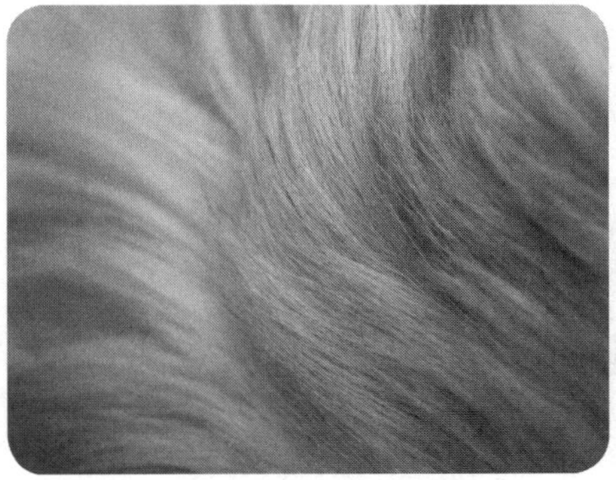

Objectives: Identify the odd one out.

Developmental Writing

Learning to Know

Trace and complete the sentences.

top

bottom

The monkey is on the top / bottom shelf.

The bird is on the top / bottom shelf.

Objectives: Use prepositions of place: top, bottom.

Follow the color code to paint the picture using watercolors.

Artistic Expression and Appreciation

Learning to Be

1 = yellow 2 = black 3 = blue 4 = orange 5 = brown

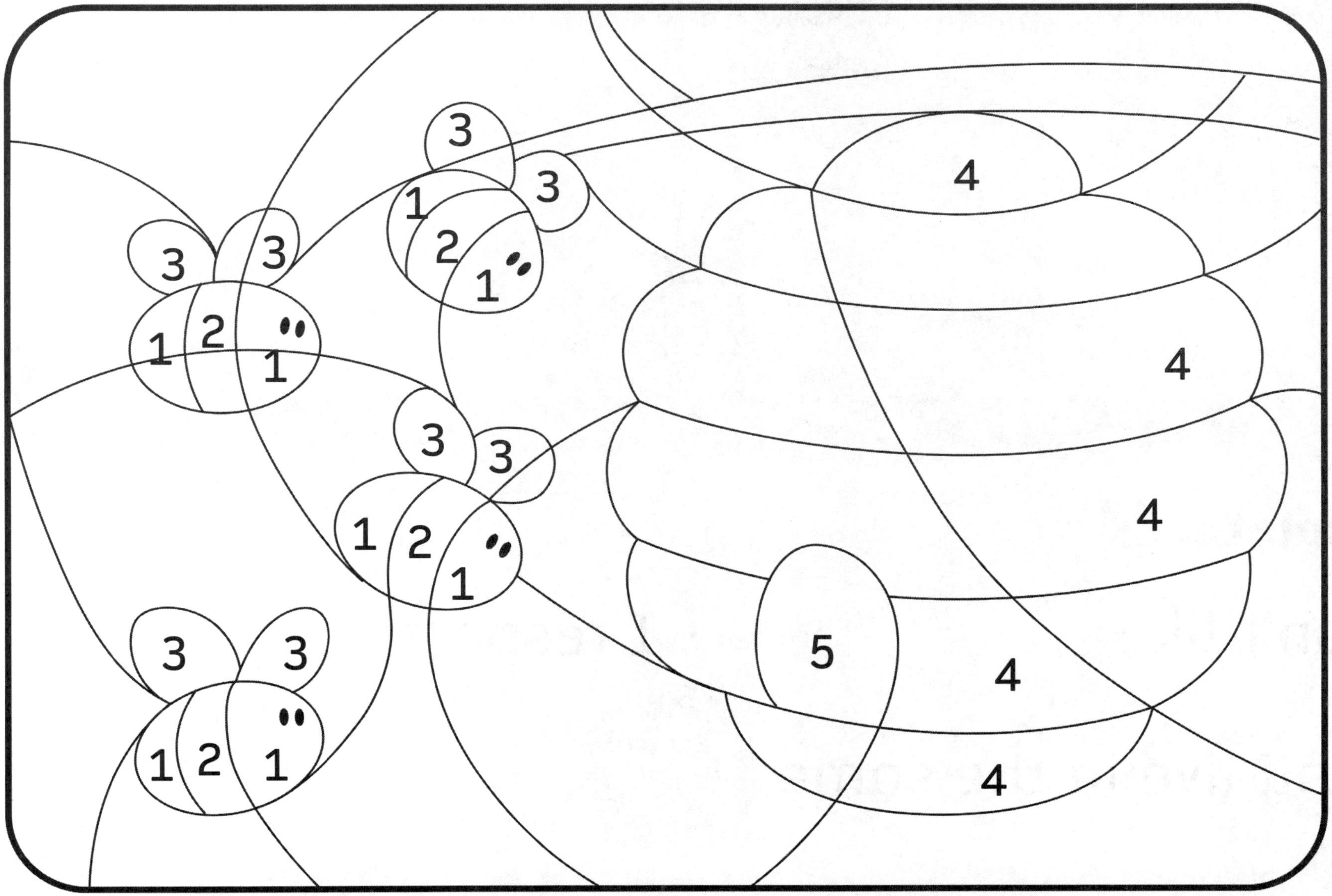

Objectives: Use different techniques to paint a picture about the natural environment.

Self-care

Learning to Be

Draw an animal you like and another one you don't like.

Complete.

I don't like ____________. I respect ____________.

We all live in the same .

Objectives: Behave respectfully towards others.

Trace and complete.

w v y w v y

Draw a word for each beginning sound.

w	v	y

Phonemic Awareness

Learning to Know

Objectives: Identify the /w/, /v/, and /y/ sounds.

Color what time you start school.

Mathematical Thinking

Learning to Know

Objectives: Read the time to the hour.

Trace and match.

Developmental Writing

Learning to Know

Cheetahs are big cats.

Cheetahs run very fast.

Baby cheetahs are cubs.

Objectives: Describe different animals and their physical characteristics.

Check.

A sick pet needs...

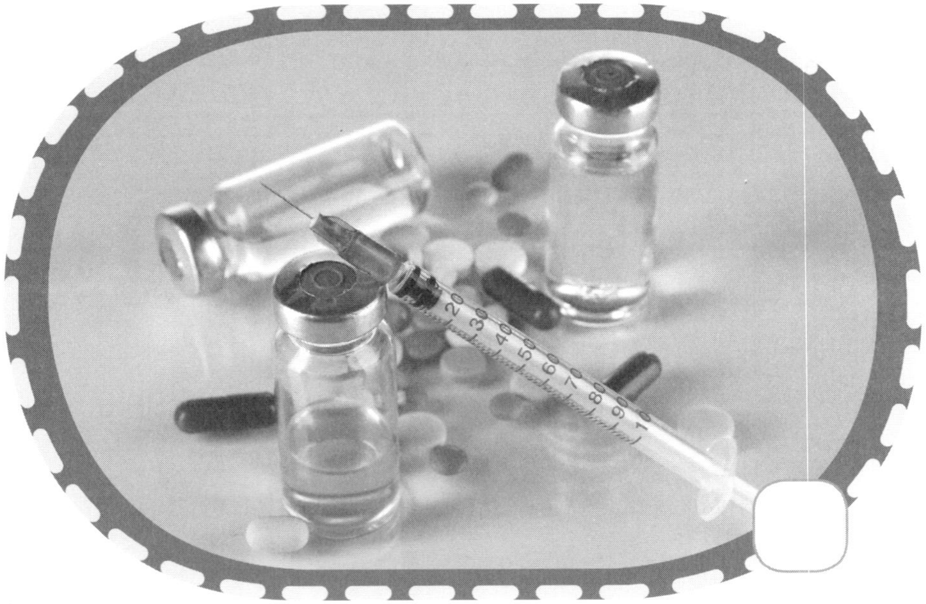

Objectives: Learn how to take care of and protect animals.

Color the kind behavior.

Objectives: Behave respectfully towards others.

Trace, count, and write.

Phonemic Awareness

Learning to Know

M

m

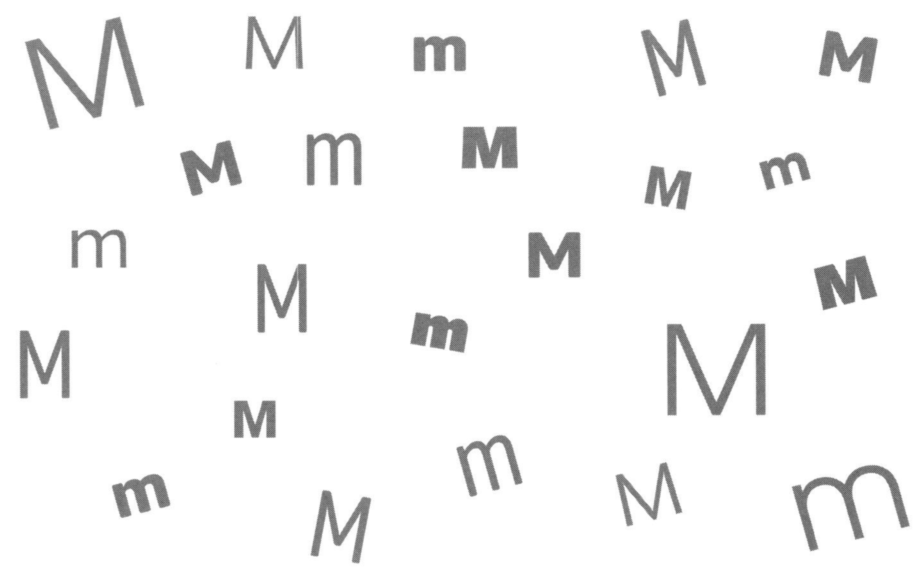

Draw two pictures of words beginning with /m/.

Objectives: Practice the /m/ sound.

Mathematical Thinking

Learning to Know

Count, color, and solve the additions.

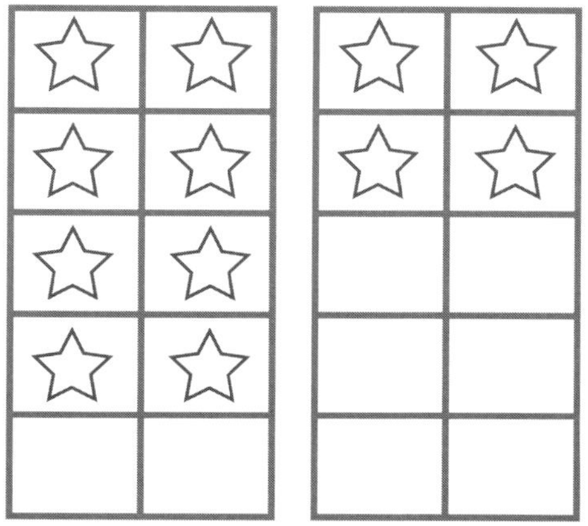

$8 + 4 =$ ____

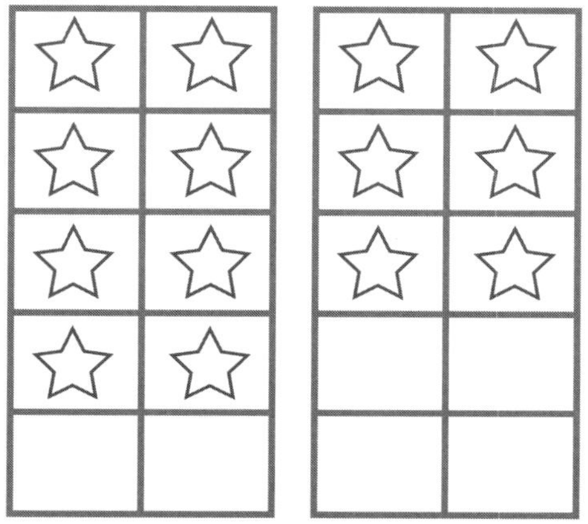

$8 + 6 =$ ____

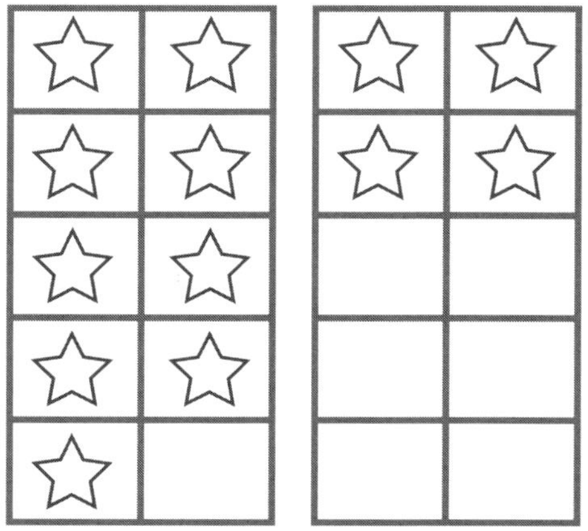

$9 + 4 =$ ____

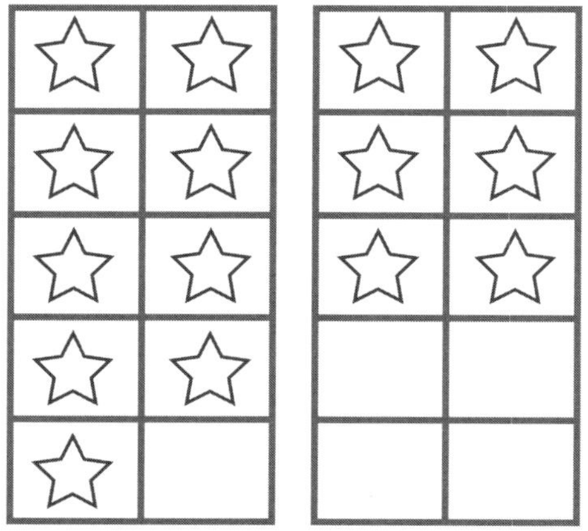

$9 + 6 =$ ____

Objectives: Solve simple additions.

Trace the words.

baker   dentist   street cleaner

Complete the sentences.

He is a ______________.

He is a ______________.

She is a ______________.

Objectives: Learn the words for community workers and places in town.

Match and color. Draw another sign and write its meaning.

Exploration and Knowing of the World

Learning to Do

silence

stop

bathroom

Objectives: Recognize everyday items found in the community.

Number the pictures in the correct order.

Physical Development and Health

Learning to Be

Objectives: Learn the importance of participating in chores.

Circle the words beginning with /s/.

Phonemic Awareness

Learning to Know

Objectives: Identify the /s/ sound.

Mathematical Thinking

Learning to Know

Look, count, and color the graph.

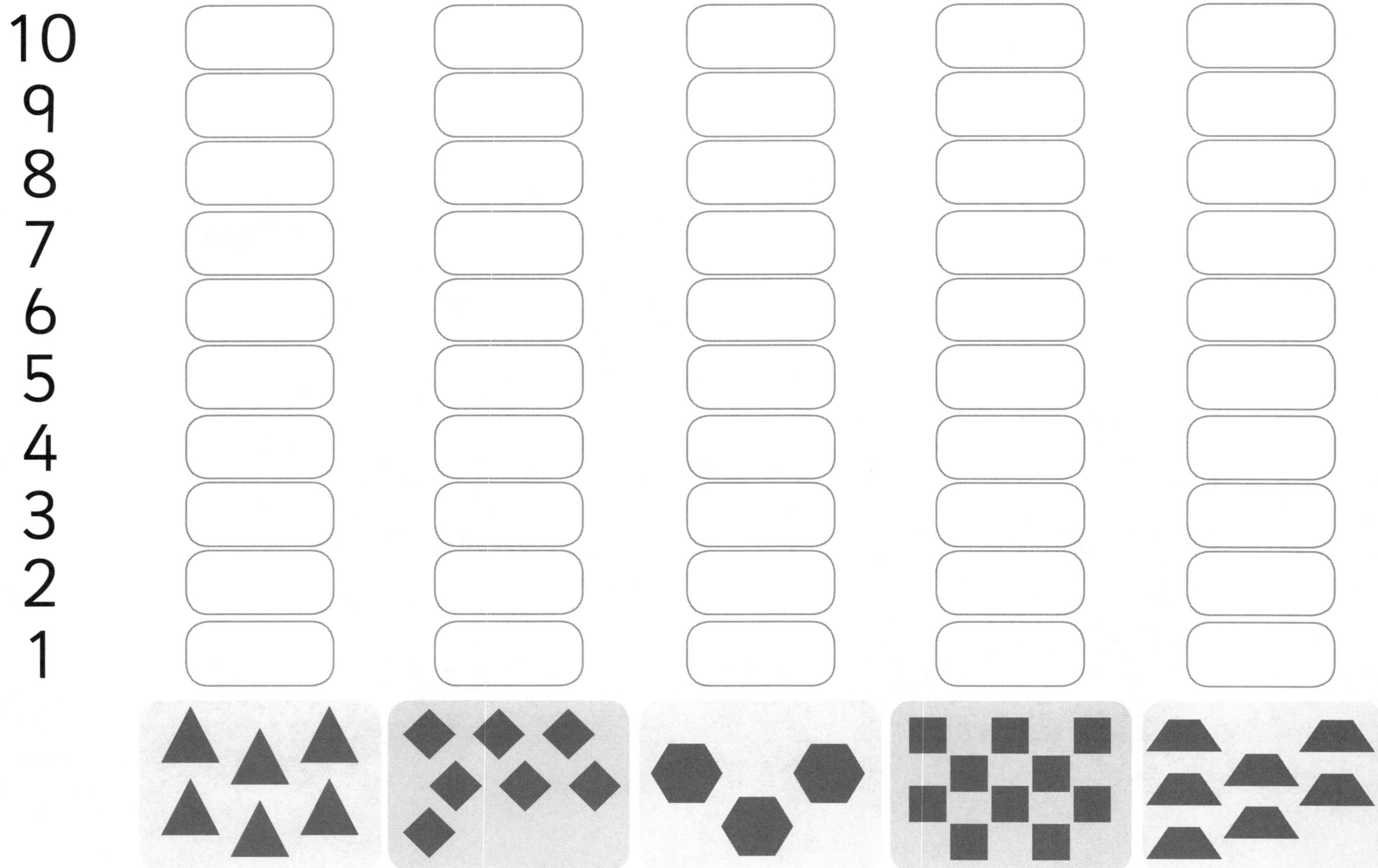

Objectives: Make a simple graph.

Developmental Writing

Learning to Know

Trace the sentences and draw a picture.

Firefighters work at the fire station.

Firefighters get on the fire truck.

Firefighters put out fires.

Objectives: Use complete sentences to describe the community workers' activities.

Make balloon faces of your family.

Artistic Expression and Appreciation

Learning to Be

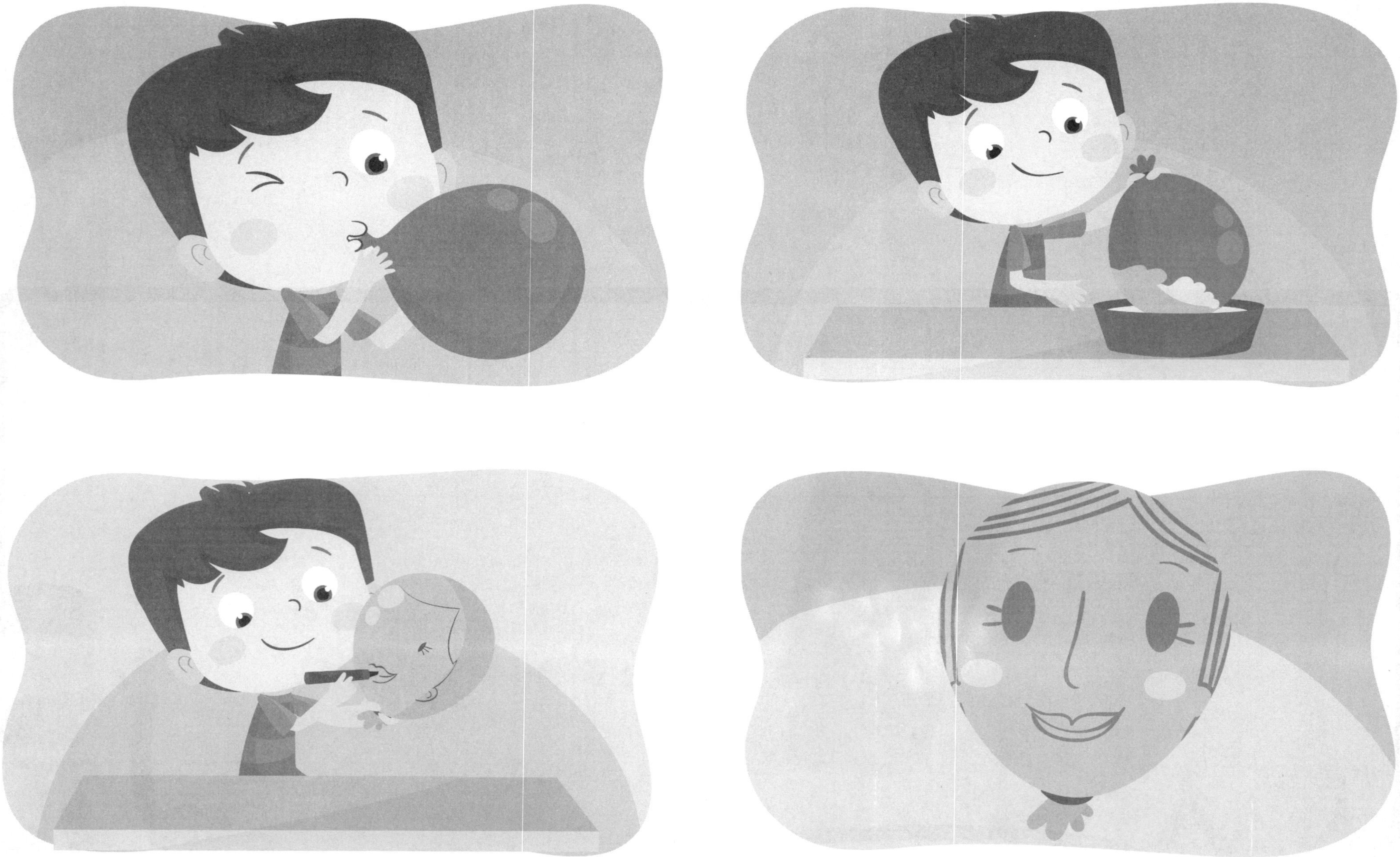

Objectives: Use different techniques to represent a group of people they are part of.

Physical Development and Health

Learning to Be

Check the groups you belong to. ✔

friends ☐ firefighters ☐ family ☐ school ☐

Objectives: Acknowledge that they are all part of groups of people.

Phonemic Awareness

Learning to Know

Complete the words with *D* or *d*.

This is Dan.
____an is a ____inosaur.

____an likes
the ____rums.

Check or cross out. ✔ ✘

Dan is a dinosaur. ☐

Dan likes the drums. ☐

I like the drums. ☐

I like dinosaurs. ☐

Objectives: Identify the /d/ sound.

Read and draw the clock hands.

Mathematical Thinking

Learning to Know

It's 1 o'clock.

It's 3 o'clock.

It's 9 o'clock.

What time is it?

Objectives: Read the time to the hour.

Trace and color. Guess the job and draw a picture.

Developmental Writing

Learning to Know

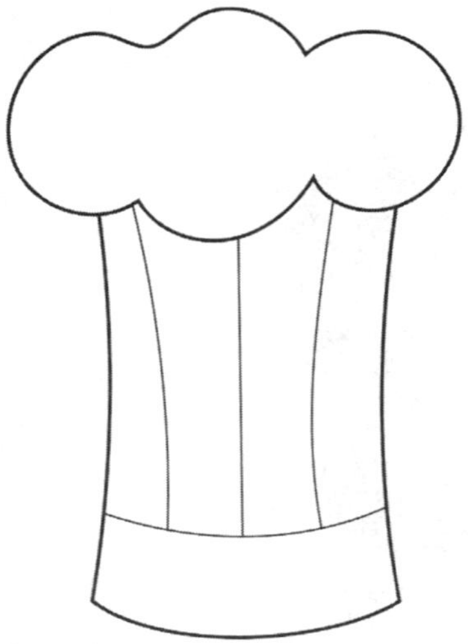

She has a big hat.

She wears an apron.

She cooks food.

She is a ____________.

Objectives: Learn key words for workplace activities and tools.

Decorate your clock. Make and attach the long and the short clock hands.

Artistic Expression and Appreciation
Learning to Be

Objectives: Make their own clock to read the time to the hour.

Draw.

Self-care

Learning to Be

When I grow up, I want to be a...

Objectives: Talk about what they would like to be.

Look and circle the words with /t/.

Phonemic Awareness

Learning to Know

This is Tessa.

Tessa wants to be a teacher.

Tessa teaches her toys.

Objectives: Identify the /t/ sound.

Mathematical Thinking

Learning to Know

Trace the names of the days. Write the month and the year.

Month: ______________________ Year: ______________________

Monday	Tuesday	Wednesday	Thursday	Friday	Saturday	Sunday

Write the numbers in the calendar.

Objectives: Write the date. Write the missing numbers in a calendar.

Developmental Writing

Learning to Know

Find the words and circle them.

t	e	a	c	h	e	r
j	a	n	i	t	o	r
d	e	n	t	i	s	t
h	y	n	u	r	s	e
d	o	t	c	h	e	f

Complete the sentences.

She is a ____________.

She is a ____________.

Objectives: Recall key words for workplaces, activities, and community workers.

Complete the street. Color.

Artistic Expression and Appreciation

Learning to Be

Objectives: Identify different public places in their community.

Literacy

Learning to Know

- **Go through the pages in this unit and complete.**

Unit 8 has ________ pages.

My favorite page is ________.

- **Draw a picture of your favorite character in the "New in Town" story.**

Objectives: Reflect on what they learned in the unit.